666 X 90

Tiger, Alpine, Rapier

Tiger, Alpine, Rapier

Sporting cars from the Rootes Group
Richard Langworth

OSPREY

Published in 1982 by Osprey Publishing Limited,
12–14 Long Acre, London WC2E 9LP
Member company of the George Philip Group

British Library Cataloguing in Publication Data
Langworth, Richard M.
    Tiger, Alpine, Rapier.
    1. Sunbeam automobile—History
    I. Title
    629.2'222   TL215.S85
ISBN 0-85045-443-3

Editor Tim Parker
Design Simon Bell

Typeset by Tameside Filmsetting Limited, Ashton-
under-Lyne, Lancashire and printed by
Butler & Tanner Ltd, Frome and London

Contents

Preface

I did not expect to be rewarded with this assignment, my second for a British publisher, and I daresay UK readers may find what follows a different approach than they are used to. This is not to imply that this or that side is better. I have a great admiration for the British motoring press, for I was weaned on Dennis May and schooled by Bill Boddy, and my run of *Autocar* is one item I must never be without.

Tim Parker, indefatigable motoring editor at Osprey Publishing in London, broached the subject of this volume several years ago, which is about twice as long as he originally gave me to complete it. I suspect I came recommended by my friend and colleague Graham Robson, who, if he keeps it up, will become the dean of his profession by the turn of the century. Tim was most polite in giving me the several extensions I eventually required, while Graham helped move my work towards a conslusion. I certainly appreciated the task—it is fun writing about cars you've owned and still respect.

I bought my first Rootes car new: a 1963 Sunbeam Alpine. This was followed by a 1966 Tiger. Both, each in its own way of course, were rare automobiles. They did precisely what the factory claimed (we all know how rare *that* is), and were built with the care and precision which had vanished from Detroit a decade earlier.

In the process of writing this book I became a Rootes owner again—twice. Within weeks of each other we landed a fine Harrington Le Mans, followed by something I thought was extinct on these shores—a 1967 Humber Imperial. But blow me even these two rare and satisfying Rootesmobiles do not seem enough, and one day I will have to own another Tiger. Selling my first one was the worst automotive divestiture since the axe fell on Alvis.

As Graham Robson was first to point out, the Rootes family should not be looked upon as the villians our champagne-quaffing brethren who drive pre-war Talbots say they are: knaves who buried the grand marques of the golden past. The Rootes simply did what was necessary, at a time of even greater economic perils than we English-speaking communities face today. They bought up defunct companies and put men back to work. And in time they began to produce some of the more interesting cars of the modern era.

Under Rootes, the great name of Talbot joined the great name of Sunbeam, and the interesting S-T 90s began to make rallying history. They ran up a series of outright and class wins in the toughest international competition, and few makes have duplicated their success since. Rootes built the pretty mid-fifties Alpines, which are still good-looking cars today, and followed with the 'new' Alpine of 1959, which is also good looking, tailfins notwithstanding. They followed with the imaginative Tiger, though somehow they missed the market analysis that should have gone with it. And they built a line of Humbers that provided good luxury in compact packages—cars that displayed their abilities on rallies as rough as the 'Monte' and the East African Safari.

An American view of the story may not be a bad idea, in fact. The Rootes Group were very much influenced by transatlantic impulses—the good ones and the bad ones. Sir William, later Lord Rootes, was already working with the Raymond Loewy organization before the war, and Loewy's team had substantial influence on what was produced postwar at Ryton-on-Dunsmore. American engineering also attracted Rootes men; they selected a Ford V8 for their Tiger in 1964 and a Chrysler V8 for possible use in Humbers during 1965. Lord Rootes admired and respected the Yanks; he came to my country often, and he preached that the USA was the 'name of the game' for British motor exports. Heaven help us, we let him down. We didn't buy his cars in the quantity he expected, and when he came here looking for a partner, who did we hand him but Chrysler? It took about three years for Chrysler's bean-counters to erase all traces of what had theretofore made Rootes products attractive to generations of enthusiasts.

But all that is well-known history and I have not dwelt upon it lengthily. This is intended to be a happy book, recording the moments when people like Stirling Moss or Peter Harper or Paddy Hopkirk drove Ryton cars at speeds they had absolutely no right to even consider, along the unearthly mountain tracks of the Monte or the Alpine, or flat-out or sideways through the long straights and high-speed corners of Le Mans and Riverside.

Not that the story hasn't been alluded to before. The late Michael Frostick wrote a fine little book on the Rootes works team in 1964, one which I unashamedly relied on heavily in outlining my presentation and providing facts. Two recent one-model books, Mike Taylor's on the Tiger and Chris McGovern's on the Alpine, are deeply researched labours of love which will become bibles on their subjects, but the whole story has never been slapped between two hard covers before. Tim Parker, whose knowledge is infinite, said it ought to be. So here it is. I hope you enjoy it.

The people who helped should be prominently mentioned— those who *wish* to be mentioned, that is, for some have preferred to remain anonymous. On the styling end, I was greatly assisted by the recollections of Raymond Loewy and his talented designers, who at one time or another contributed to the Rootes programme —Clare Hodgman, Bob Bourke and John Reinhart. The works competition stories which dot the manuscript with bright natter and inside poop came primarily from Lewis Garrad, Norman's son, who served constantly wherever the works team ventured, and has a razor-sharp memory to boot. From California, Lewis's brother Ian assisted; and in Georgia, author Gregory Wells kindly gave me permission to quote from his fascinating 'driveReport' on the Sunbeam Tiger in *Special-Interest Autos*. Thanks too to *SIA* editor Dave Brownell, who also gave his blessing.

The photo research would have been a dead loss without the assistance of Tom Ansell, technical receptionist at Atlas Photography in London—repository for Rootes photo archives covering 1935–70. Tom presented us with marvellous indexes to a ten-foot-high stack of files, without which we'd still be there looking. In the National Motor Museum at Beaulieu, photographic librarian Peter Brockes dug into his archives, and head librarian Nick Georgano responded to numerous questions and ran quests on my behalf. Over in Sussex, my friend Michael Sedgwick bored into his files for help with production figures, and constantly lent his encouragement.

Graham Robson's efforts on behalf of this book and myself could not be listed in a hundred pages. He began by recording a long interview with Lewis Garrad; he compiled all the specifications for Sunbeam and Humber; he read and critiqued every word of the manuscript; he located the Atlas people and got filthy helping me research photographs; he liaised with Mr. E. M. Lea-Major of the PR department at Talbot UK Ltd; and he wrote the appendix on Hillman Imp rallying. (My file on the Imp consisted only of Bob Fendell's comment that he could keep his rally Imp going by stringing a wire over his shoulder to the carburettor when the linkage broke.) A large percentage of what is contained herein, then, is entirely due to Graham Robson. I cannot begin to express my thanks to him for saving me from myself, for helping make the book as accurate as possible, for being so tolerant of my faults, and for being, in short, such a good friend.

Richard M. Langworth
Hopkinton, New Hampshire, USA
31 July 1981

I

The Roots of Rootes

'Melancholia assails us all—some more than others—often to the detriment of sanity and reason. Ah, how sweet they were, the days of Bugatti and the carrozzeria of ye olde country! We order up another Pimms No. 2 and reflect on the dismemberment of old excellence.' Captain Ralph Stevens, a Maine-based autoholic, was talking about the disdain levelled at MG TFs when he wrote that lovely paragraph—but he could equally have been referring to Rootes-built Sunbeams, Humbers, Hillmans and Singers. Rarely has the vintage crowd in Britain stopped to consider those cars on their own merits, preferring instead to mourn the loss of great vintage-era marques.

'Quality, like connubiality in the human female, is a state of mind,' Captain Stevens concluded. And the state of mind of most graduate enthusiasts leans towards blaming the Rootes brothers for wrecking grand names with production-line pish-posh. If rebutted with the suggestion that Sunbeam, say, wouldn't have survived the thirties were it not for Rootes, the common reply is that this indeed is what should have happened, rather than the denigration of the Sunbeam badge. But the argument is fallacious: what sometimes issued from the production-oriented Rootes Groups were cars worth more than a casual glance, even if they did not set any Land Speed Records. And that is what this book is all about.

Both British and American readers may be interested in the parallels between the Rootes family (William and Reginald, with their sons Geoffrey, Brian and Timothy) and the Stateside Studebaker family (Peter, Clem, Henry, Jacob and John, all brothers), a few generations and 4500 miles removed. Like the Rootes, the Studebakers entered the motorcar trade from an allied industry: bicycles for the British family, wagons in the case of the Americans. The cycle operation began in 1902, under the direction of William Rootes, Sr., in Hawkhurst, Kent. It was from there, after the First World War, that young William and his brother Reginald entered the retail automobile trade in the twenties and became manufacturers during the thirties. Rootes Ltd was formed in 1932, and by

Devonshire House, in London's famous thorough-fare, Piccadilly. This was the Rootes Group's headquarters from the end of the 1920s to the mid-1960s

1936 they controlled the destiny of Hillman, Humber and what had formerly been Sunbeam-Talbot-Darraq. The Singer Company were brought in during 1955, formalized in January 1956.

Scanning the relatively sparse material on the Rootes family, one is further reminded of the Studebakers in descriptions of their character. For both were of a stock we have all wonderingly known: strong, decent, bluff, shrewd, hearty. This can perhaps be accounted for by the way of life and heritage of their parts of England and America, or even by the possibility that more favourable climes may conversely darken and convolute the native personality. An American newspaperman, describing one of the Studebakers, might have equally been talking of Sir William Rootes when he described his subject as 'a genial man with a highly suspect hayseed air. "I'm just a country boy," he will say disarmingly, but there is something about him that makes a city slicker count his fingers after a handshake.'

Young Billy Rootes (we shall occasionally use his nickname, which he retained even after being knighted, to distinguish him from his father) was sent from Hawkhurst to Cranbrook School, and then to Singer in Coventry—one supposes he jumped, in 1955, at the chance to absorb his former employers—to learn the motor trade as an apprentice. His younger, more introverted, cautious and quieter brother Reginald, meanwhile, followed a business course, being educated in the intricacies of administration and finance. After the First World War the two moved from the cycle to the motor trade with a successful chain of retail car outlets in Kent. In the early twenties they relocated to Long Acre, London, and in 1926 moved to Devonshire House, Piccadilly, which remained Rootes headquarters throughout the period described herein.

The first Lord Rootes who, as 'Billy' Rootes, founded a great motor-manufacturing dynasty

William and Reginald were a perfect combination. Graham Robson has written that Billy 'wanted to be as important, and as wealthy, as Herbert Austin and William Morris'. He was several decades behind those two great pioneers, of course, and he realized he would have to work his way into their league by acquisition, rather than invention. Billy's skills, Robson continued, 'were as a salesman, and as a motivator of men; Reginald . . . was the administrator. As William was later to say on many occasions, he might be the power unit of the Rootes Group, but Reginald was the steering and brakes. The one had the bright ideas, and was for ever dashing off in a new direction, while the other made sure they could all work, and restrained his brother from excesses.'

By 1928, the Piccadilly operations had become so successful that Rootes were the largest motor distributors in Britain. Simultaneously there arrived Billy Rootes' opportunity to do more than just sell cars. Hillman and Humber were—conveniently—in financial trouble; even more conveniently, their Coventry factories were close together. Hillman in particular had had a bad time of it after the war. Some years before the Rootes brothers beckoned, its managers had discussed selling out to Siegfried Bettmann, who ultimately bought Dawson and launched the Triumph car in 1923.

In this action one may recall yet another American parallel: the effort by crack sales executive Joseph W. Frazer to 'buy control' of a functioning manufacturer during and after the Second World War. Frazer ultimately obtained Graham-Paige, and allied that firm with Kaiser-Frazer. Detroit car makers scoffed at this upstart who proposed to become one of them. 'Frazer never built a car in his life,' they said, 'he just sold them.' Similarly the advent of Billy Rootes was greeted with hoots by the moguls of Coventry, who could hardly imagine a less likely candidate for their as yet still rather exclusive club. With the arrival of the Rootes family—their initial entrée was as large shareholders, not outright owners—the former Hillman and Humber hierarchy rapidly disappeared. Spencer Wilks and Captain (later Sir) John Black, joint managing directors of Hillman, immediately departed—Black shortly to join and then to lead Standard, Wilks later to direct with distinction the fortunes of Rover. One can understand the rationale here; the motorcar business is a serious game, and its leaders in that time of a near *laissez-faire* business climate were generally hard-driving and forceful in disposition. It is inconceivable that Billy Rootes and John Black could have been partners in any venture.

The only fly in this apparently promising Rootes ointment was a little matter known as The Crash. Wall Street plummeted in October 1929, the American economy with it, duly followed by the rest of the Western World's. The Rootes family, already faced with sales problems involving weak 14hp and unhappy straight eight Hillmans, and an expansive but slow-selling line of 9, 14 and 20hp Humbers, were immediately thrown into the problems of a slack economy and a reeling motor industry.

The Hillmans were restyled for 1929 and priced as low as £295, and Rootes encouraged every attempt to increase production. But by 1931 the Hillman-Humber combine was in even worse straits than 1928, facing either liquidation or reorganization. At this point the Rootes family stepped in to assume full control, formally created the Rootes Group and embarked on a programme of model revision and line rationalization.

For Hillman especially, the Rootes connection couldn't have come at a more opportune time. William and Reginald soon convinced Captain J. S. Irving of 'Golden Arrow' fame to direct the creation of a new small car, designed to weld with the thin wallets of the Depression-era British public. The result was the 9.8hp Hillman Minx, with a solid little 1185cc side-valve four-cylinder engine which developed 25bhp at 3600rpm. The chassis price was only £120, and there were two models, a four-door saloon at £159 and a tourer at £198. The Minx was not a great car—what Hillman ever was?—but it was certainly a good one, and fair value for money. Through 1933 the Minx was accompanied by the larger 2.1- or 2.8-litre Hillman Wizard, but this model didn't sell well and the Rootes rationalized it out of existence by 1934. Later large Hillmans inexpensively deployed the big Humber engines.

The Hillman Minx of 1931 was the one single car which put the Rootes Group on the way to massive growth. It was nothing special in engineering terms or styling, but simple, cheap and reliable

A significant departure for the Hillman Minx was its production technique—a streamlined, mass-volume operation. Billy Rootes had studied and admired the bung-'em-out practices of GM and Ford in North America; later he would strive mightily to exploit the US market with his own car.

The Minx did nothing but improve during the Thirties. A four speed gearbox and optional free wheel and radio were offered for 1934; a progressive all-synchromesh transmission arrived a year later and the 1936 restyle brought a GM-like integral boot. The all-synchro gearbox vanished after 1939 for cost reasons, but in the short-lived 1940 model year the Minx adopted unitary construction—a new and relatively unique idea for a car of its class at the time.

The first sign of the sporting Rootes cars to come was the Hillman Aero Minx of 1933, on a shortened 78in wheelbase. Though its drive train was straight out of the standard Minx, its chassis was distinctly different, being underslung behind the front spring brackets and fitted with long, almost flat rear springs. Bolt-on engine mods included a high-compression cylinder head and down-draught carburettor fitted to a modified exhaust induction system and a remote-control mechanism afforded a short gear lever. Though Hillman proclaimed that this chassis was mainly intended for specialist coachbuilders, the stock coupé design, with its rounded, sloping radiator shell and integral stone guard, was handsome and popular. Prices were £145 for the bare chassis, £245 complete. In 1934 Hillman added a sports four-seater at £225 and a close-coupled foursome saloon at £255.

The Aero was a dashing addition to a line of cars whose more standard models were in no way sporting, and in concept was a portent of the future. The Rootes family were hard-headed businessmen first, enthusiasts a very distant second, but if the market was there, they *would* consider derivations of their standard models. This proved to be the prevailing philosophy from the acquisition of Talbot in 1935 through the Ford V8-powered Sunbeam Tiger of 1964.

A few historians have pointed out the essential truisms about this period of Rootes consolidation and absorption. In doing so they became almost 'revisionist historians' in that they were re-justifying, *vis-à-vis* the complaints of the enthusiasts, what was perfectly justifiable in the thirties. Bluntly, men were out of work. But Britain was climbing out of the Depression by 1934, and Rootes helped put people back on the job. The firms they had added to the Hillman-Humber empire—Thrupp and Maberly Coachworks (Rootes-owned since 1925), Karrier in 1934, Clement Talbot in 1935, British Light Steel Pressings in 1937, the Sunbeam Motor Company in 1938—were all struggling, and the struggles were mainly due to the Depression or bad management. The great Louis Coatalen, remember, had borrowed half a million pounds in 1924, a ten-year loan to finance his Grand Prix endeavours. That note fell due in the very depths of the Depression, and Sunbeam, of course, could not pay up. As Karrier, Talbot and Sunbeam entered receivership in the thirties, Rootes picked them up, promising marketing know-how and new, mass-production techniques, supported by the formidable financial resources of Prudential Assurance, their largest backer. Thanks in part to a slowly recovering economy, Rootes succeeded. Against production of about 5000 cars per year in 1930, they built a capacity of 50,000 per year by 1939. Rootes, along with firms like Rover and Standard—were partly responsible for making Coventry, by the outbreak of the war, 'Britain's Detroit'. As such, they contributed vastly to the wartime production which enabled Great Britain to withstand the onslaughts of Nazi Germany, until those who had hitherto been half-blind were half-ready. For their wartime efforts both William and Reginald Rootes were knighted, and they well deserved the honour.

Rootes were firmly convinced that Coventry was the place to build cars. The offer to run—for a suitable fee—shadow factories built and paid for by the British Exchequer, was irresistible. In 1936 there was no guarantee that war with Germany would ensue, and the big plants did not convert from cars to aircraft engines. Everyone hoped peace would reign forever—but few hoped as hard as the auto-makers.

Accordingly, once Rootes gained control of Sunbeam, the latter's factory in Wolverhampton was sidelined in favour of a shift to Coventry. The company also began operating a shadow factory, built close to their Hillman-Humber plant at Stoke Aldermoor. Then, in 1940, the huge shadow complex at Ryton-on-Dunsmore was opened, just outside Coventry on the London Road. Rootes moved in—to build aircraft engines for the duration and cars afterwards. Ryton, along with most other former shadow factories, still builds cars today. It is now the headquarters of the Peugeot-controlled Talbot Company, successors to Chrysler, successors to the Rootes Group.

With the absorption of Sunbeam and Clement Talbot, William and Reginald set out to build, first, a quality line of conventional cars and, second, a sporting confection capable of exploiting the good names they had inherited. In this they achieved the unremitting enmity previously mentioned. The last Talbot designed by Georges Roesch, the magnificent 3.5-litre '110', was out of production by 1938. With the Rootes takeover, Roesch was set to work designing a 'Talbot Ten', essentially an updated version of the Hillman Aero Minx. This car duly appeared for 1936–39, replacing the previous Talbot 65, which had gradually been gaining more and more components from the Hillman production line. Sunbeam, acquired three years after Clement Talbot, did not field a range of cars for 1938. But the next year there issued forth a new marque—Sunbeam-Talbot. On this unlikely base rests the origins of the postwar sporting Rootes cars.

Geoffrey Rootes, 'Billy' Rootes' eldest son, who became the second Lord Rootes when his father died, and who also became the company's chairman for a period in the 1960s

Bernard 'BB' Winter, Rootes's much-respected engineering chief in the 1940s and 1950s, who managed to interpret the wishes of the Rootes family in a very practical way

The Sunbeam-Talbot Ten was indeed a quality product. It had always, *The Autocar* noted in August 1939, 'been noted for its excellent finish, and all exposed chassis details [including the wheels] are now stove-enamelled so as to afford the greatest possible protection against corrosion. Liberal use is also made of sound-deadening material. . . . Indeed, this new range of Tens should enhance the reputation of the marque as a small car of quality. [The Ten] is known not only as one of the prettiest cars on the road, but also as having a lively performance, which it is capable of maintaining for long periods without loss of tune.'

With the Sunbeam-Talbot successfully launched for 1939, Rootes set about developing a sporting derivation for the following year. Four '1940' models were duly created: sports saloon, drophead coupé, sports tourer and roadster, priced from £248 to £285. The open cars resembled in form the earlier Triumph Gloria four- and two-seaters, while the saloon was little altered from the rounded, roomy shape that had appeared for 1939.

Considerable attention was, however, paid to the new chassis. The 1940 frame was slightly wider, to better support the coachwork, and tubular cross-members were now found welded to the main frame members, to improve rigidity. Another change was the use of piston-type Luvax shock absorbers, attached differently than in 1939 and vastly upgrading the handling. An interesting

At a preview of the Hillman Super Minx model in 1962, Britain's Prime Minister, Harold Macmillan (far left), talks to John Panks of Rootes about the car. Panks is now chairman of the Automotive Products components group

PREVIEW OF THE LATEST FROM ENGLAND

the all NEW HILLMAN SUPER MINX

THE IMPACT CA

The best of the *IM*ports

coupled with

the best of the Com*PACT*

Available With Fully Automatic Transmission

George Hartwell (left), whose inspired production of the two-seater Sunbeam-Talbot 90 led to Rootes building the first Sunbeam Alpines of 1953

detail appeared on the 1940 range which would become a Rootes trademark after the war: the hand-brake lever, instead of being fitted between the front seats, was set into the offside sill panel, where it allowed one to hold the brake with one hand whilst adjusting the choke or engaging a gear with the other. With variations such as floor mounting outboard of the driver's seat, this would be a Rootes feature for the duration of the Group's life. Another Sunbeam-Talbot innovation was the use of metric equivalents on the instrument dials. This too persisted through the 1960s, though it was perhaps less important then than it is now.

The small six craze—for providing high-performance via under-2-litre sixes that didn't much affect taxable horsepower—had waned by 1939. But the idea of big-engined little cars hadn't, and Rootes took due note of it. Anticipating that 1939 Motor Show which never came, Sunbeam-Talbot announced a 1944cc side-valve four-cylinder 'Fourteen' as line-mate to their 1185cc Ten in August 1939. This car was mounted on a longer, 96.5in wheelbase, though at 2250lb it weighed little more than the Ten. And, just as the pre-war Sunbeam-Talbot Ten would evolve into the postwar Sunbeam-Talbot 80, this powerful 2-litre would find its way into the Sunbeam-Talbot 90.

The new Fourteen (actually, RAC horsepower was 13.95) was similar in design to the Ten, but much faster, its pounds/cc ratio only 1.16:1. *The Autocar* deemed it 'quiet and smooth [capable of producing] useful power without being stressed'. Their road test revealed a 0–60mph sprint of 22 seconds through the gears and a top speed of 80mph—impressive, in 1939, for a car costing less than £300.

At a prize-giving in London are Gilbert Hunt (*right*)— who became managing director of Rootes in the 1960s following the Chrysler takeover, and Lord Rootes, the company's chairman

The picture tells its own story. Thrupp & Maberly was a well-known independent North London coachbuilding concern until taken over by the Rootes Group in the 1930s, and after that it looked after the manufacture of the more specialized and sporting Rootes products

'Average speeds', the test reported, 'can be high. This is due not only to the fast natural speeds of the car and its quick acceleration, but also to lightness and general ease and facility of control. Corners can be taken without appreciable reduction of speed, the car holding a steady course, and also the brakes are entirely equal to the performance capabilities. . . . The suspension is of a soft type, giving a high degree of riding comfort.'

Once again, with this new Fourteen, Rootes were demonstrating the lessons they had learned from the people in Detroit, where numberless variations and models were offered by the simple expedients of engine and body swaps. For the 2-litre four powering this new Sunbeam-Talbot was in fact nothing new at all, but the same engine used in the Hillman 14. And the Hillman 14, to carry the General Motors formula to a typical conclusion, shared many body stampings with the Humber Snipe, Super Snipe and 16.

Alas, that 1 September issue of *The Autocar* also contained forbidding news from the Continent: British motorists on holiday or business abroad had been 'recommended to return immediately'. In that last weekend of peace for six long years, over 2200 cars had queued up at the Channel Ports to be shipped home, most of them forever. The Sunbeam-Talbot Fourteen and an Austin Twelve were the last cars to be tested by *The Autocar* before the war, and Rootes' promising future was brought up short by international developments.

What might have happened to the marque in the years immediately following must be left, of course, to conjecture. Would these semi-sporting Sunbeam-Talbots have taken readily to the rally circuits of 1940, 1941 and 1942? Or would Donald Healey, who worked at Ryton-on-Dunsmore for a time (and who recalls dreaming about a Rootes-based sporting car), have been allowed to express his considerable genius in Ryton instead of Warwick? We cannot say. All thoughts of motor sport, indeed new cars in general, were laid aside by the momentous events of 1939, and it was not until much later that sporting Rootes cars would emerge, under the guidance of newer hands.

2

Sunbeam-Talbot: only a lovely name?

Rootes' share in Britain's war production was characterized by Geoffrey Smith of *The Autocar* as 'amazing', and this was no exaggeration. In 1939, Rootes Group companies employed some 17,000 workers; by 1945, one in every 100 of those in the war industry were working for the country through Rootes. The shadow factory scheme, which had involved Rootes earlier than most other companies, had been in operation since 1936. 'Back then', Sir William Rootes said in 1945, 'we had not the slightest knowledge of the aircraft industry and no small sacrifice was involved. We diverted some of our best executives and most skilled craftsmen just when competition in the car industry was at its fiercest.'

The result of Rootes' strong effort was rewarding, however. Their factories made about one out of every seven bomber aircraft in the United Kingdom, built fighters and modified 2700 aircraft under rush conditions to suit changing battle patterns. With their former competitors, Rootes factories overhauled over 21,000 Rolls-Royce Merlin, Bristol Pegasus and Hercules aircraft engines, 'many so damaged as to need complete rebuilding'. In addition, they built some 300,000 bombs and five million bomb fuse parts; assembled over 20,000 imported Army vehicles and repaired about 12,000 more; overhauled 9000-plus service vehicle engines; supplied three million all-metal ammunition boxes and a million aero engine spares; and trained over 11,000 Army personnel in mechanical schools. Rootes' share of armoured car production was 60 per cent; of scout car production, 35 per cent. Overall, Rootes contribution to the British war effort was 11 per cent of the total volume of all wheeled vehicles combined.

If, in 1945, the Rootes brothers were thinking that the government owed them something, they probably were justified, though they didn't ask for much. They wanted an equitable postwar tax rate and adequate supplies of raw materials—two items which the postwar Labour government was notoriously reluctant to grant. But despite government-decreed austerity, things looked promising in 1945. Two of Britain's chief export rivals—Germany and

FNX 883

With World War II just over car production started up again in Britain with most manufacturers concentrating on pre-war designs. This is a 1946 Sunbeam-Talbot Ten. A modern successor was sorely needed

Japan—were prostrate; the Empire was still intact; the worldwide need for manufactured goods was staggering.

At a luncheon at Claridge's in January 1945, Sir William told listeners that he would not lead them 'up the garden path' about 'any imaginary dream cars'. When the Government gave his company the go-ahead, there would be a speedy flow of cars which, he said, would look like 1940 cars, but be quite different under the skin. The postwar Hillman Minx had just been proposed with 54 important improvements, based on wartime experience. All-new cars would furthermore be in the offing as soon as the industry hit its stride. Later Rootes said that Britain should not settle for 500,000 vehicles a year, but 1.5 million—which the industry didn't reach until 1963. The opportunities were there, he said, and British industry would be foolhardy to ignore them. (Where are you, Lord Rootes, now that they need you?)

As for his own company, the chairman was as good as his word. When the first cars began trundling off slow-moving production lines in late 1945, they proved to be much the same as those seen before the invasion of Poland six years earlier. Still, the Rootes brothers had continued their programme of rationalization begun in the early thirties.

In the original companies absorbed by Rootes there were 22 different base models; by the end of the war these were reduced to four: Hillman, Sunbeam-Talbot and two Humbers (though the S-Ts and one Humber offered a choice of two engines each). Gearboxes had formerly numbered 10; now there were just two. Engines were down from 13 to three.

The pre-war-based Sunbeam-Talbot Ten and 2-litre were produced from 1945 through 1948, using their old 1185cc and 1944cc

Confirming the adage that motoring fun can be had in any car—this 1946 2-litre Tourer competes with bravado on the 1952 Brighton Rally. S-T still had a sporting name

side-valve fours, mounted on wheelbases of 94 and 97.5in respectively. Saloons, dropheads and tourers were offered in each range, with 1946 prices running between about £650 for the Ten tourer to £850 for the 2-litre drophead, inclusive of purchase tax. (This was a formidable amount of money in 1946, and, coupled with severe petrol rationing after the war, combined to raise Billy's hackles on more than one public occasion. Sir Stafford Cripps was no friend of the Rootes.) Talbot remained completely incorporated with Sunbeam, and was never considered as a separate postwar make; it was enough of a headache just producing the S-Ts. (The larger, Humber-engined models from before the war did not reappear.)

The Ten and 2-litre effectively stopgapped the immediate postwar need, but anyone half as dynamic as Billy Rootes would know that a modern successor would soon be required. Accordingly Rootes set in motion the design project which resulted—in 1948—in the first truly postwar Sunbeam-Talbots, cars that would make the hyphenated marque respectable in the eyes of sporting motorists. The styling of these automobiles, which came to be called the S-T 80 and 90, is of interest to enthusiasts on both sides of the pond, for it involved not only Rootes talented body engineer Ted White, but none other than the expatriate French designer long resident in America—Raymond Loewy.

When some American GIs dragged a French soldier named Loewy off the First World War battle line and deposited him at a medical unit, they were saving one of the major talents of the industrial world—and the talent had been showing for some time. Born in Paris in 1893, Loewy had designed a foot-long model aeroplane in 1908, and even formed a company to manufacture it. He entered college to study electrical engineering, but the war intervened. After being patched up he shipped himself to America with 40 dollars in his pocket, completed his education and set out on a career in commercial art. A Loewy design for Macy's department store in New York caused an uproar—because it was clean, rather than cluttered. Loewy left Macy's, vowing to be his own boss whatever the future assignment.

Raymond Loewy's strikingly simple yet elegant designs would continue to cause uproar years later, in the cluttered age of American and European car styling. There was no reason, he would say to audiences in the mid-fifties, for fads—chrome-plated or otherwise. Loewy disparaged chrome, whether on the face of a Chrysler Town & Country or a Rolls-Royce Silver Cloud. He despised excess weight even more. 'Weight', he declared, 'is the Enemy. My whole automotive career has been devoted to proving that point to disbelieving manufacturers.'

Loewy's big career 'break' came in 1929, when he redesigned the Gestetner duplicating machine—his first big contract. The new design lasted 20 years. Soon Loewy's services were sought for projects from toothpaste tubes to electric shavers, cars, buses, aeroplanes, ferryboats and ocean liners. Before the Second World War, the Royal Society of Arts awarded Loewy their Royal Designer to Industry diploma—the first time this honour was conferred on a non-Briton in the Society's near-200-year history.

Forming a large industrial design firm in the thirties, Loewy remained prominent in his field. His highest achievement, he says, was being retained as consultant in the US space programme, which caused him to be invited to participate in the Soviet space programme as well, though this he declined. Loewy has strongly affected everyday existence. Today, if you drive your 1981 Avanti II to the post office, fill the tank with BP or Shell on the way, wash down a snack of Oreo biscuits with Canada Dry ginger ale and light up a Lucky Strike cigarette, you'll have come in contact with six Loewy-designed packages or logos within the hour.

Loewy has always loved cars—driving and racing them as well as designing them. His first production design was for Hupmobile in 1934. One of the prettiest Hupps in history, this was an aerodynamic car based on a custom that had won Loewy a grand prize at Cannes two years earlier. The Hupp was noticed by several other car manufacturers. One of these was Studebaker's Paul G. Hoffman, who signed Loewy up as a design consultant in 1937. Loewy's association with Studebaker lasted, with an interregnum of eight years, from 1939 to 1963 and he and his firm were directly responsible for such watershed designs as the 1939 Champion, the 1947 Starlight coupé, the 1953 Starliner hardtop, the 1956 Studebaker Hawks and the 1963 Avanti.

Another manufacturer interested in Loewy's ideas was Billy Rootes, but here the relationship was nowhere as close as it was between Loewy and Hoffman. By the time Rootes and Loewy were

Readily posed styling drawing, blue print and model of the new 1950 Sunbeam-Talbot 90 drophead coupé shown at a special exhibition at the South Bank, in London

introduced, the latter had built a large and very busy design firm, with offices in New York, Palm Springs and Paris. Loewy could not be everywhere at once, but he could—and did—recruit the best talent in the field to assist him. One of these assistants, who would play a key role in postwar Sunbeam-Talbot design, was Clare E. Hodgman, who was assigned to Loewy's London offices after the Rootes contract was secured in 1938.

Hodgman, who now lives in Florida, had broken into the design field in 1931 at the age of 17, with the General Motors Art and Colour Section. Under the legendary Harley Earl, Hodgman passed a fruitful apprenticeship; he went to Loewy in 1937. After the Rootes contract became official in 1938, Hodgman went to London

1948 Sunbeam-Talbot 90 four door saloon, the first of the line. The Loewy influence is obviously strong. Rear wheel spats have to be removed to change a rear wheel. The 80 was virtually similar

to establish Loewy's offices there. He left when the war started, and quit Loewy in 1940 to go to Sears, Roebuck. But Loewy hired Hodgman back in August 1945 and sent him back to London to renew work on the Rootes account.

'The Loewy–Rootes connection was suggested by a mutual acquaintance of both gentlemen,' Hodgman told the author. 'He knew Rootes well and was a personal friend of both. As I recall, Mr Loewy was not too involved with Rootes after the contract was negotiated, he had relatively little contact with the Rootes brothers.'

Why was Sir William Rootes so intent on styling input from an American firm? 'This was the Rootes brothers' policy,' Hodgman explained. 'They wanted an American influence in their cars, something that would be fresher than what they had in England at that time. Lord Rootes was very American in many ways; if it wasn't for his accent you'd think he was an American promoter. I don't use that word disparagingly, I mean he was more of a flamboyant salesman-type than you'd expect—very liberal in his ideas, very progressive. The fact that he got into the aircraft business so long before the war shows that he knew what was going on. He was always enthusiastic, creative, trying new ideas. Reginald was the man who actually ran the business. It was a wonderful team; they rounded each other out. I liked and admired both of them immensely.

'We had very little influence on Sunbeam-Talbot design before the war. After we reopened the London office, though, we got to work in earnest. There was too much to do at Studebaker for me to reside in England permanently. Instead I would go over at least once a year, and would stay a month or six weeks. The Rootes brothers were very keen about design, and so was their chief engineer, B. B. Winter. It was Mr Winter who kindly insisted that they would have no contract with Loewy unless I supervised the designs. I had 10 to 14 people under me at home, but on the Rootes assignment I had only one assistant, a clay modeller loaned from the Studebaker project. In Ryton, we worked with the Rootes body design team of body engineers, headed by Ted White.

'Everything we created for Rootes was done on quarter-scale clay models, fashioned in the States. These would be taken over on our annual trips, and then Ted and his people would put our quarter-scale clays into full-size shape. When they had those done I would come to England, and we might make a couple of modifications. When a prototype was completed, it would be taken out on a grassy area of seven or eight acres, surrounded by a high fence. There we'd all look at the car under daylight conditions, which was very informative. I think this was a "first" for both sides of the pond. Detroit didn't have outside viewing areas until much later, even at GM.'

Ted White himself related in later life that he had personally been inspired by aircraft forms in the design of the postwar Sunbeam-Talbots. The wing shapes, for example, were prefigured by fuel drop tanks on wartime aircraft. Aeroplanes were a transatlantic influence on postwar car designers. GM's Art & Colour Studio, for example, was at this time perfecting what became the 1948 'tail-finned' Cadillacs, with inspiration from the Lockheed P-38 twin-fuselage fighter plane. Bob Bourke, Clare Hodgman's associate at Loewy (and later partner in an independent firm), admits to being strongly influenced a few years later by the Lockheed Constellation passenger aircraft in creating the timeless 1953 Studebaker Starliner.

Clare Hodgman is at pains to point out that the Loewy influence was not the determining factor at Rootes, and that he worked very closely with Ted White in making styling decisions: 'Ted was a nice man, very co-operative. There was never any friction or any problems, and he was most helpful. It was a fine working combination, and we were fortunate to have someone like him to interpret what we were trying to do. Ted's studio was under the direct supervision of Mr Winter's Engineering Department, as were many styling groups in those days, and without his interpretation between our pure side and the engineers, we would have been far less pleased with the cars that resulted.'

Raymond Loewy has always taken pride in designers like Clare Hodgman, but he has also insisted their every action was an interpretation of his guiding philosophy—simplicity, lightness, function. Whether or not Loewy personally played a role in the postwar S-T designs, the cars that evolved must have merited his approval. Like the postwar Studebaker, the new Sunbeam-Talbots blended traditional and modern concepts, retaining individual front wings, but sweeping these smoothly into the body at the front doors. Indeed, what came to be called the Sunbeam-Talbot 80 and 90 were even more streamlined than the revolutionary 1947 Studebakers, because there were no bolt-on rear wing assemblies: the body just flowed smoothly back into a simple, rounded tail. This Rootes shape, which would last in various forms until as late as 1957, was one of the most individual and predictive of the day.

The 90 chassis, at announcement in 1948, was simple but effective. The engine is tall. Our photograph was stamped 'With the compliments of Public Relations. Rootes Securities Ltd.' Leaf springs all round

Hodgman recalls that Reginald Rootes played a significant role in design evaluations: 'I can recall that he insisted on larger, more comfortable seats. And the doorline had to be designed so that he could get his outside foot in without hitting the edge of the front door. He was very meticulous, as was his custom, and was an important influence on Ted White and myself.' Hearing this the author asked Mr Hodgman if Sir Reginald had been responsible for Rootes' uncommon outside placement of the handbrake, which occurred on pre-war and many postwar models. 'Probably not personally,' Hodgman said. 'After all there were others, like Bentley, who did that for years and years. I think it was possibly more of a tradition, and a good idea.'

Loewy's people at Studebaker never had to contend with one British tradition that exercised dominant styling influence on the 80 and 90: the upright, classic radiator grille. 'We tried a lot of fresh things after the war to get around that,' Hodgman said, 'but tradition prevailed and they changed things around on me. The upright grille was one of these. Sunbeam and Talbot—separately—had been great traditions in England, and neither they nor I wanted to destroy history completely. The grille was the sort of thing you couldn't mess with, like the Packard radiator. Keeping it was one of the "givens". [Accepted restrictions of the job in hand.] Of course, Rootes were completely free to veto any idea of ours. We gave them lots of different things in that relationship and they took what they wanted.' Retaining the grille was also good business. It gave buyers a visual reference with the past: it was distinctive and —carefully blended into the long, curved bonnet of the car— looked good.

Rootes summed up their 80 and 90 four-door saloon as cars which introduced 'the new art of *streamstyling*. This original conception, the new thought in automobile design in accord with the

25

Stark contrast between American-styled 90 saloon and 'old English' house. Rootes Motors knew of the good sense to show off their most modern design to its best effect. Compare this side view with that on page 23. This is a Mark II

modern age, conveys what is self-evident to the eye—graceful power and modern appearance. The traditional supremacy [thanks to that grille] of Sunbeam-Talbot in the design of sports cars is reaffirmed.' This flush-sided styling, Ted White and Clare Hodgman have both pointed out, was quite an innovation. The 80 and 90 were among the first flush-sided cars in England.

Rootes' 'streamstyling' was carried deftly through at the rear; where the wheel cutouts were covered by spats, or skirts. The pillarless rear door/quarter window junction of the old Ten and 2-litre was retained; the tail-lamps and rear number plate nacelle were flush-fitted; door hinges were concealed and door handles were pull-out types. The boot lid lifted from the top backwards, carrying a felt-lined tray that housed a complete tool set. The boot, though a bit difficult to reach, was commodious.

Interior styling of the 80 and 90 was very American—even to the extent of a column-mounted gearchange, though this might have been suggested by long-legged Reginald Rootes. John Reinhart of Loewy, who was sent over to Coventry now and then to help Clare Hodgman, takes credit for the dashboard: 'It was my only contribution,' he told the author, 'but I was generally happy with it. It conveyed all the necessary information clearly and without elaboration.' (Reinhart had also designed the ultra-modern facias of the 1947 Studebakers.)

The dash panel carried horizontal ribbing for most of its width to give a unified look. No polished walnut was used. A central radio nacelle and ignition-cum-control buttons were in the centre; two bulges at each side housed a large glove box and the instruments. The speedometer, wrapped around the steering column, was easily visible through the sprung steering wheel. As usual speed was conveyed in both Imperial and metric measurements. Similarly the smaller gauges—fuel level, clock, amps and temperature—which flanked the speedometer. Sub-facia air ducts kept a supply of fresh air moving through the cockpit. Detail niceties included quick-

A contemporary Rootes showroom somewhere in the Midlands, perhaps in Northampton. The year is 1952 or 1953. Postwar austerity is not exactly overflowing here. Dealer is lucky to represent Rolls-Royce and Bentley too. This shot shows that apart from the lack of an out-and-out sports car the Rootes range was reasonably well balanced

action window cranks, detachable concealed rear ashtrays, a rear armrest and a wheel control for front seat adjustment.

Two models were offered in both the 80 and 90 series: a four-door saloon and a drophead coupé by Thrupp and Maberly. The latter was hammered out at T&M's premises on Edgware Road, North London, from unfinished saloon bodyshells. The bodies were built by British Light Steel Pressings in Acton; Rootes 'sourced' the engines to the former Hillman-Humber works at Stoke in Coventry. The 80 was priced on introduction at £889 for the saloon and £953 for the drophead; the 90 was approximately £100 dearer.

The mechanical package was not immediately up to the cars' fine styling. The chassis (except for engines, the 80 and 90 were identical cars) was simply the old 97.5in wheelbase affair from the old 2-litre, which was anything but modern with solid axle and semi-elliptic leaf springs front and rear. The steering was the old worm and roller type. All these components, incidentally, were also straight out of the concurrent Hillman Minx, and the chassis design was easily 10 years old. About the only new item was that column gearchange—and 'four on the tree' has never been a very good set-up, nor was it praised at the time.

27

A 1951 publicity shot, again of the latest Talbot 90. The radiator side grilles and under-headlamp side lights denote Mark II. Humber Hawk in the background

The powerplants of the new cars looked different, with overhead-valve cylinder heads, but underneath were the old 1185cc Hillman Minx engine (80) and the 1944cc unit from the Humber Hawk/Hillman Fourteen (90). The 1185 had first appeared on the 1931 Minx; the 2-litre could trace its lineage back to the '32 Humber Twelve. The 90's 2 litres, Rootes literature put it hopefully, would provide 'vivid acceleration and hillclimbing, fast average cruising speeds over long distances and impressive all-round performance with complete dependability'. Dependable maybe—but road tests showed 0 to 60 taking 26.8 seconds, the standing quarter-mile 22.5 seconds and the 90's top speed just nudged 80mph. The 80 could barely exceed 70mph, and *its* 0–60 time was 36.4 seconds. (A point of interest was that the 80's camshaft was on the offside and the 90's on the nearside—which caused Kent Karslake and Ian Nickols to suggest that this contrast had the makings of quite a good song!)

In fairness it should be pointed out that Rootes *did* engineer

Here's the drophead 90 in 1951. Once more the contrast between sleek smooth lines of the body-shell and the thatched cottage is intentional

improvements into both engines, the 2-litre particularly. Its 64bhp at 4100rpm was 15 per cent greater than the old 2-litre's output. Although the 90 weighed more than the 2-litre, it was quicker in both acceleration and top speed. (The latter is partially owed to the fact that it was also more aerodynamic.) Both engines used special Lo-Ex light alloy pistons, which had an empty groove for an extra ring to be inserted if, after many miles, it was required. These and other changes—like chassis reinforcement in critical spots—were what Sir William meant when he talked about detail improvements postwar buyers would never notice in their warmed-over pre-war machinery. But the styling *was* postwar, and it was good. That was proven by sales.

If traditionalists were still mourning the pre-war double loss of Talbot and Sunbeam, they didn't represent the buying public. Sales of the 80 lagged—Rootes dropped it in 1950—but the 90 was very popular. Both Ryton and North London worked to full capacity through the early fifties, bunging out saloons and drop-heads, but much early production was targeted for export markets and there was a real shortage of 90s in England.

Still, what we had at this point was a nice-looking car without very much suds. Thus the introduction of the Sunbeam-Talbot 90 Mark II, in late 1950, for the '51 model year, may be considered a watershed in the marque's history. The Mark II was not only a fine automobile in its own right, it was the basis of the successful Rootes Works Team.

Styling changes were minor in this 90 Mark II, but they did exist. To comply with minimum headlamp height requirements in certain export markets, the front wing curvature was altered, raising the headlamp height by 3in. This revision also moved the headlamps slightly farther apart than before. The Mark I's built-in passing lights, carried low on each side of the radiator grille, were eliminated in favour of flanking, horizontal-bar grilles. Small, round parking lamps were added under the headlamps.

Much more important were the mechanical changes: a completely redesigned, very rigid chassis frame; independent coil-and-wishbone front suspension; hypoid (instead of spiral) bevel rear axle and increased displacement through a bore increase, which yielded 2267cc and 70bhp at 4000rpm. These improvements were what made the Sunbeam-Talbot 90 into a rally car to be reckoned with.

Aside from cylinder bore the engine was not greatly changed. It retained its three main-bearing crankshaft, Lo-Ex light alloy pistons with extra notch, chain-driven camshaft with harmonic cams and pushrod-operated overhead valves. But rally experience with the Mark I had shown that the car was susceptible to heat build-up in its fairly cramped engine bay. Accordingly a new, more efficient water pump was applied to the Mark II, incorporating a block-type thermostat, which eliminated the need for external water pipes. The new flanking grilles also assisted cooling.

Mark II chassis. Not many changes over that shown on page 25 except for the coil sprung front suspension and diagonal cross-bracing. Gear lever is still 'on the tree'

The change from spiral to hypoid bevel gears was accompanied by a direct-drive ratio of 3.9:1 instead of 4.3:1, and the indirect gears were also somewhat higher. This, and the six extra horsepower that resulted, helped boost the 90's top speed to 86mph and reduced its 0–60 time to 24 seconds. Other important details included a variable-ratio steering gear and thick rubber bushes to decrease vibration transmitted from both engine and gearbox.

The new independent front suspension encompassed lateral short upper and long lower wishbones. The lowers, hinged near the centre of a large cross-member, were triangular in plan view, and hinge bearings were widely spaced to provide longitudinal rigidity. 'They are inclined rearward at the extremities so that the axis of the hinge on each side, if prolonged, would meet in the centre of the car,' a press notice stated. The upper wishbones were mounted in hollow brackets above the cross-member ends. 'The top of the bracket forms an abutment for the large coil suspension spring on each side,' the press release continued. 'The outer ends of the wishbone are linked together by a yoke which carries the swivel pin for the stub axle of the front wheel. Armstrong double-acting hydraulic spring dampers are employed. . . . A torsion bar couples the two and controls roll.'

Two more generations of 90 followed the important Mark II: the Mark IIA, for model years 1953–54, and the Mark III, produced for 1955–57. (The Alpine roadster, which ran from 1953 to 1955, will be covered separately.) Successive improvements were rendered with both Mark IIA and Mark III, but not all the changes were above criticism.

The Mark IIA was a mild evolution of the Mark II, with certain styling revisions: open rear wheel wells and perforated instead of slotted road wheels. Mechanically, the first IIAs differed only in the use of wider brake linings. But by mid-1953 they had adopted a higher-compression cylinder head (7.42:1), which delivered 77bhp at 4100rpm. Even this wasn't enough; the 90, it must be said, was never quick in 'stock' form. It always suffered from weight, the inevitable result of cramming in as much luxury as possible—something of which Raymond Loewy, perhaps, would have disapproved. But added horsepower did give the IIA a genuine 80mph capability, and nipped about three seconds off its standing start 0–60 time.

The Mark III appeared in late 1954 with more horsepower and torque—80 at 4400, 122 at 2400 respectively. It still weighed close to 3000lb, but it was now a genuine 91mph motorcar, and its 0–60 time of 18.4 seconds was more than acceptable for 2.2 litres at the time—especially one that returned 24 miles per gallon. But there were other, more obvious changes on this model that displeased many enthusiasts.

It was noticed right away that the Mark III was simply labelled Sunbeam—Talbot had completely disappeared. Undoubtedly this move stemmed from the fact that the new Alpine two-seater, introduced the year before, had also deleted the Talbot suffix, probably for readability. But there are those who suggested that the Brothers Rootes killed the wrong name: 'A Talbot Alpine (with memories of those fantastic performances by the 105s in 1932 and 1934) would have been more appropriate,' wrote Graham Robson. 'It was the last we would hear of Talbot until the late 1970s, though I have no doubt that a hale and hearty Georges Roesch was quite relieved to see it happen.'

There were other changes on the Mark III that inspired the occasional raised eyebrow. The frontal aspect had become more glittery, with large flanking grilles filled with thick vertical bars, fully encompassing the parking lights. The Mark III was a few inches longer due to larger, heavier bumpers, and it sported Buick-like extractor portholes along the sides of the bonnet. These had a

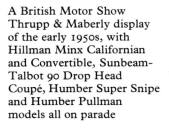

A British Motor Show Thrupp & Maberly display of the early 1950s, with Hillman Minx Californian and Convertible, Sunbeam-Talbot 90 Drop Head Coupé, Humber Super Snipe and Humber Pullman models all on parade

practical purpose—improving still more the engine cooling characteristics—which was more than Buick's portholes accomplished. But it was hard to stomach for some, even if Rootes did alter the dashboard to provide for a centrally mounted, optional rev counter. And on top of it all stylists added perhaps the ultimate insult—duotone paint jobs.

The Loewy people are willing to take the blame for the two-toning. 'It was our idea,' Clare Hodgman remembered. 'This was the kind of thing that was "American" and the Rootes liked the idea because they never had it before. Others didn't. They were very set in their ways. For instance, they couldn't understand why the Americans would build a two-door sedan instead of a four-door. They rarely built them and couldn't comprehend why we did. But that's "tradition". The two-toning took a few years to get deeply rooted into their conception. The British are extremely nice people. It takes years to be their friends, but once you are, you're friends forever.'

In Hodgman's defence the duotoned Mark III was tastefully done. The idea of applying a second colour over the roof and bonnet/bootlid surfaces has resurfaced recently (or maybe never really died), with good workouts on both American and European luxury cars. It was the Rootesmobiles of the later fifties, with their garish body two-toning at which Britons had more reason to look askance. And they, too, were the ideas of the Loewy group.

The minor specification changes on the Sunbeam Mark III were more the result of continued rationalization within Rootes than attempts at higher performance. The cylinder head, for example,

Times have changed. Three model girls in someone else's garden show off the Mark III Sunbeam drop-head. Whitewall tyres and dummy side vents are all the rage. The door doesn't appear to fit. Date 1955

A year later in 1956 for this Mark III Sunbeam 90 saloon with two-tone contrasting paint. Rootes took to two colours and stayed with them for years. The conservative British weren't easy to convince

was now similar to that used on the Humber Hawk, with compression raised a touch (from 7.42:1 to 7.50:1) and the inlet valve diameter was increased from 1.55 to 1.63in. Intake and exhaust ports were altered. Separate exhaust ports were now provided for all cylinders, instead of siamesing numbers two and three. On both saloon and drophead (as well as the Alpine roadster) a new Stromberg D136 carburettor was used, with a manual instead of automatic choke. A useful Mark III option was Laycock de Normanville overdrive, controlled by a switch under the horn button, operating on top gear only. Overdrive required a shorter driveshaft and a 4.22:1 instead of 3.9:1 rear axle ratio, so these Sunbeams had a deal more flexibility, being quicker off the line and quieter at high speeds.

This fascinating combination of British and American product planning was the raw material on which the Rootes Competition Department was based. It is all they had to work with, with the late exception of the Alpine. Although the soundness of the product cannot be faulted, there could have always been something better —a lighter saloon, for example, or an alternative to that clumsy column-mounted gearchange. These were, for their day, heavy, luxurious, rather costly cars, not always characteristic of rally champions. Yet champions they were, thanks mainly to a former Talbot man who would make Sunbeam-Talbot a name to excite enthusiasm as in days of old: a canny Scot named Norman Garrad.

3

Of Alpines and Montes

Norman Garrad had joined Clément Talbot Ltd in 1934 as a sales representative in the north of Scotland, so when Rootes acquired Talbot in 1935 it also acquired Garrad. Norman retained his Scottish sales position until the war, but his real interest was in competition. Even before he took the slot at Talbot he'd been immersing himself in the classic motorcars of Georges Roesch. When a team of Talbot 105s won the Coupes des Alpes in 1932 without one penalty mark, car number 9 was driven by Garrad. Talbot repeated this performance in 1934, so Norman must have been delighted to enter into sales promotion of their cars—and suitably chagrined when the whole Talbot operation was absorbed and then closed down by Rootes. But he stayed with the new owners. During the war, Garrad served with the Third Armoured Division, from which he was released in 1945 with the rank of Lieutenant-Colonel.

Talbot's great heritage, says Norman's son Lewis, 'suited him exactly. He was proud of the rank of the car. He set rather high standards, and often got cross with his sons. During the war I was a corporal, my brother Ian a lance-corporal. He didn't really go for that. We could have been London postmen.'

After the war Garrad returned to Scotland for a year, then moved to Ryton-on-Dunsmore as Sunbeam-Talbot sales manager. In this role he served through 1949, when Rootes changed his position to head of Sales Promotion. By then, however, he'd become so involved in competition that he spent little time on sales.

In Ryton, Garrad interested himself in making the Tens and 2-litres more like their Talbot forebears—or as much like Talbots as they could be. 'The first rally car I can remember coming home was a Sunbeam-Talbot 2-litre,' Lewis said, 'a pre-war model which he used in the Land's End Trial. This car had been specially modified—they'd taken the front wings and air cleaner off of it and had bound the rear springs in string.' Crude, but it worked: 'He brought the cup home, and we thought that was fantastic, that he'd won the World Championship.' Garrad's efforts at rally preparation

Norman Garrad (Sunbeam-Talbot 90), ready to start the French Alpine Rally of 1949. His was one of the Team Prize winning cars

were at first solitary, so he deserves credit for engineering this initial victory. Nobody at Rootes knew anything about competition. Garrad was the father of it all.

Despite his minor victory in Cornwall, Norman Garrad looked askance at the immediate postwar Sunbeam-Talbot models. Author Michael Frostick reported in his 1964 book, *Works Team*, that Garrad considered the 2-litre (which he also drove in the first postwar Alpine Rally) 'exceedingly dangerous to drive fast down the mountain passes because of serious brake fade. Fuel starvation, tyre problems and inadequate shock absorbers had all proved problems, and the 2-litre's gear ratios were ill-chosen for rally work.' Remarkably, Frostick noted, these criticisms did not fall on deaf ears: 'Bernard Winter ("B.B.", Rootes, competent director of engineering) listened with some sympathy to what Garrad had to say. Brake-lining manufacturers were consulted and Mintex produced the M.20 lining after various different brake drums . . . had effected only a partial cure. Similar experiment was carried on with the shock absorber settings, petrol pipes were moved to avoid the heat of the exhaust and the gearbox was redesigned to give better-spaced ratios.' Of course these steps were taken gingerly. It wasn't until the arrival of the new Sunbeam-Talbot 80 and 90 in 1948 that Garrad began to carve out the Rootes Competition Department.

Norman Garrad liked to take the latest S-T model on the Alpine Rally every year, and in 1948 he used his first 90, a late prototype. His sponsor was the company house organ, *Modern Motor Travel*. Another 90 was entered by racing driver George Murray-Frame. Frame took a Coupe des Alpes, but Garrad suffered sump damage

and finished low. As with the 2-litre, Norman took his complaints about the 90 to Winter, who improved sump protection on later production cars.

'I recall this incident,' son Lewis remembers, 'in that father came home and said, "I can do the mods just as well myself." He then set up a sort of competition shop in a part of the sales department, back of a paint shop at Stoke. In this he was assisted by mechanic Jimmy Ashworth, test driver Glen Johnson and two other mechanics. One was Jerry Spencer; the other I remember only as "Big Ray". The first thing they wanted was to find some more power in the thing, and suddenly we had senior engineers polishing heads and crankshafts, balancing pistons, and all the rest of it. On reflection, you know, it was amateurish.'

Maybe so, but its significance should not be lost. Garrad was essentially pioneering the whole postwar approach to competition by mass-producers, which would result in some of the most exciting motor sport in history—and which still goes on today. Pre-war, the successful competition cars were mainly hand-built, low-production sports models. Postwar, they were 'cooking' versions of ordinary cars taken right off the assembly lines. This was a revolutionary change, not even realized at the time it was happening. (It is incidentally the reason why Sunbeam-Talbots were at first sniffed at by the *cognoscenti* as bastard rigs of Hillman and Humber bits.) Garrad was also proving, to a volume manufacturer, that competition really *did* improve the breed. B. B. Winter, and more important Sir William Rootes himself, soon realized the potential of such activity. The latter backed Garrad with cash.

'Most of the money for the project came from Rootes,' Lewis Garrad stated. 'Lord Rootes was a believer in promoting the flag— he insisted that Union Flags be put on all the rally cars. So this was an official project, in that a budget was set up to develop and enter the cars. Yet the whole department at this point was nothing more than father and the aforementioned chaps, plus B. B. Winter.'

As time went on and the operation became more involved, Garrad began to farm other fields of finance, notably Shell Oil and the component suppliers. 'There was Shell money in the competition department, definitely,' Lewis continued. 'Dad would do

In the 1949 French Alpine Rally, this team of 'Mk I' Sunbeam-Talbot 90s won the coveted Team Prize, driven by Norman Garrad, Peter Monkhouse and Douglas *The Autocar* Clease

Stirling Moss's 'works' Sunbeam-Talbot 90, high in the Alps on the 1952 Alpine Rally, and . . .

. . . works Sunbeam-Talbot 90 at work, in the Alpine

a Motor Show—he used to call them "the breadline". Then he'd go and have lunch with the Shell man, come back and say, "I've got X number of pounds". Next day he'd have lunch with the Dunlop man and have Y more pounds, then lunch with the Laycock man, and so forth. He would really go around. I don't think there was actually Shell money in the Rootes business, though. For years Rootes never recommended any other oil, but I think this went back to Lord Rootes. He had been a Shell dealer when he started, and once he made a deal with someone he never burned them.' Thus, off in a corner but reasonably well financed, Norman Garrad rolled up his sleeves.

Step one was engines. Lewis Garrad remembers that they relied here on a mechanic named Ernie Beck: 'He stuttered, and we called him "cold starter". He was anything but that. Ernie would literally take a car off the assembly line, completely built, take out the engine and start rebuilding it. He would go to the polishing shop— all we had was the old belt-driven equipment—and get the thing polished, then balanced and crack-tested. We never gave him any orders. He knew exactly what to do.

'Once we'd decided, right, we have the engine to rights with Ernie's expertise, we'd decide on the details. For instance, we wanted two fuel pumps because we thought that was the thing for reliability. Then we spent a lot of time going up to Betws-y-Coed in North Wales. We'd take a car up on Friday morning and if it

broke, back to the drawing board. There was an awful lot of what I term seat-of-the-pants engineering. We couldn't go out and buy expertise, because there was none to buy.

'I remember that we were having trouble with gearboxes overheating going up hills. A chap came round from Engineering and said, "It's simple—just drill a hole on that mainshaft and that will pump the oil out." What he meant was to put four little holes at each end so the oil went in at the back, was centrifuged up the shaft, and came back again. Elementary, but it worked. That solved our gearbox problem.

'We went like that, hand to mouth. Steering arms were breaking, steering columns were seizing up, cars were overheating. When we had a problem, we had to put it right. I say 'we' because at that time I had started my pupilage, and was by devious means plotting to get into the competition department. They had a funny rule at Rootes—you couldn't be directly responsible to your father. So I was employed by the Service Department, and that, operationally, was assisting in the back-up and fixing of the cars. I ended up doing the homologation, which was a bit of a joke. I had a chap named Ernie Breech [no relation to Ford's Breech] who used to go down to London. He'd suggest things to the RAC to get the homologation accepted as we wanted it.

'It was a tremendous time to be there, because we were talking about developing cars from the wheels up. But the things that used to break were unbelievable. Can you imagine rear springs? Track rod arms? This is not poor comment on Rootes' production engineers. They had a tremendous amount of work on their hands productionwise, and they were really sticking their necks out. They weren't sure whether rallying or racing was going to work for them. But there was a tremendous amount of good will towards us from all the departments—especially after we started winning.'

Back to 1952, Moss finishing the driving test at Cannes, and gaining his first Coupe des Alpes. Moss was already something of a 'young hopeful'

The original-style Sunbeam Alpine of 1953, showing off its really elegant tail profile

The Sunbeam Alpine of 1953–55 had a really capacious, if rather shallow, boot

Win they did, but not immediately. A team of three 80s was entered for the 1949 Monte Carlo Rally, driven by Peter Monkhouse, Nick Haines and George Hartwell. While Monkhouse finished fourth in class and 31st overall, his fellows ended up thirty-seventh and forty-sixth. Norman Garrad decided to put his emphasis on the 90, commencing with the Alpine Rally the following summer. This time Monkhouse and Hartwell teamed up to produce a fifth overall, followed by Douglas Clease (twentieth) and Norman himself (twenty-fifth).

For the 1950 Monte, the Sunbeam-Talbot 90s won a prize for the 'best non-French team' (Citroën took the team prize), being 'the only eligible marque with three cars intact' at the finish. Individual showings were not as good as 1949: Monkhouse was highest in forty-sixth place, with Garrad/Cutts sixty-sixth and

Pearman/Chipperton sixty-eighth. In the same rally, however, other Rootes forces were heard from. Garrad and company had been tweaking the Hillman Minx and the new Humber Super Snipe. The Minx won the 'best-equipped' prize—the Humber, driven by a Dutch team of Maurice Gatsonides and K. S. Barendegt, finished second overall!

The weather, which had been uncharacteristically mild in 1949, was its usual unspeakable self in 1950. Louis Chiron arrived home in Monaco to deliver a soliloquy on the travails of icy roads. Gatsonides announced that he and Barendegt had survived 'thousands of phenomenal avoidances'—yet they'd brought the

1953 Sunbeam Alpine with fashionable across the bonnet strap in leather. MKV 21 registration plate suggests that this is a 'works' car as do the chromed headlamp stone guards and Union Jack beneath the windscreen pillar. Outdated trafficator 'slot' looks incongruous

Stirling Moss' 'works' Sunbeam Alpine, with no time to spare on the summit of a *col* in the 1953 Alpine Rally. He was on his way to a second Coupe des Alpes. That is snow on the ground —in July!

Standard publicity shot (familiar background) for the Sunbeam Alpine taken in 1955. A genuine 100mph car with good luggage room, at least for two, was a rare beast in the early 1950s. Twinned Lucas spot and fog lamps are fitted up front

Humber home without a single penalty mark. There were only four other mark-free cars: a 3.5-litre Hotchkiss, driven by Becquart/Secret, and a trio of Simcas.

Had Gatsonides outrun Becquart's Hotchkiss in the Mont des Mules regularity test, he would have won the Rally going away. Alas, the French car proved unstoppable. Maurice's Humber, *The Autocar* noted, 'was at a disadvantage on a circuit involving many sharp hairpin bends'. Still, second place overall was an impressive showing for a competition department which hadn't even existed three years before.

The estimable Monkhouse sadly died during the 1950 Mille Miglia, so Garrad called in Gatsonides as team captain for the 1950 Alpine. The great Dutch ace was first in class, with George Hartwell second, at the halfway mark. Then fate interfered. Gatso's rear axle packed up, and poor Hartwell collided with a Citroën in Switzerland. Though he remained on the scene and administered first aid to an injured passenger, he was stopped at the border when frontier guards actually fired at him to keep him from flying through in the normal Alpine manner. He arrived at Cannes an hour late.

Yet more unfortunate was a third Rootes driver, Murray Frame, who made all the controls on time only to have his battery fail in Monte Carlo, and cost him the Coupe des Alpes. Exemplary of the Rootes team's precision was the way they'd kept him in the running. His battery had actually begun giving trouble the last night out—the team kept him on time by stopping at pre-organized points and juggling batteries from car to car!

Despite the disappointments, 1950 was an encouraging year. Not only had Garrad honed the rally team to a fine edge—there

Two of the six Sunbeam
Alpines used in the 1953
Alpine Rally, such a
successful event for Rootes

was a new car in the works. The ifs Mark II 90 was moving towards
production, and its specification implied great things for rally work
in the 1951 season.

Evolution of the classic Mark II Sunbeam-Talbot 90 has been
covered in the previous chapter, but it is useful to note the changes
it wrought from the competition standpoint. The Mark I had
already provided an immensely strong chassis frame, and Garrad's
men had wrung reliability out of it. What the Mark II gave them
was a far more sophisticated package in detail. It was no lighter—
indeed it was heavier—but its ifs, added horsepower and variable-
ratio Burman recirculating ball steering more than made up for its
poundage. Its body, too, had received alterations bred from rally
experience—improved ventilation via small flanking grilles in the
wing aprons, where the fog lamps had previously been built in.
The Mark II's big, comfortable seats and near vertical steering
wheel were helpful on long-haul competition work. The fact that
the gear lever was still on the column was perhaps less important
than latterday enthusiasts might think—the drivers seemed to
handle it well enough. The Mark II was higher geared than the
Mark I, undoubtedly at Garrad's urging. These changes made it
much more competitive. It is not surprising that the marque became synonymous with rallying with the advent of the Mark II,
and it was now the choice of many a private entrant.

For the 1951 Monte, Garrad teamed with Basil Cardew in a 90,
Gatsonides led the team again, and one R. P. Minchen of the
Metropolitan Police showed up in the big Super Snipe. Gatsonides
was the man of this particular hour, winning the best-equipped
prize. Garrad was in America during the 1951 Alpine, but a 90
driven by John Pearman and John Cutts finished third in class,

despite a lot of over-2.5-litre competition. George Hartwell, driving another Mark II, was only 0.6 second off his scheduled class speed for the Mont Ventoux hillclimb, besting—among other things—an XK 120; this brought Rootes the Mont Ventoux Cup. Then came 1952, Stirling Moss and the finest Rootes performance to date.

Born in 1929, both his parents having motoring backgrounds, Stirling Moss was a natural competitor. He broke into racing with Formula 3s in 1948, winning 10 events that year and eight—including his first foreign win at Zandvoort—in 1949. Moss was British Champion at the age of 20, and already the subject of great expectations when Garrad signed him to the Sunbeam-Talbot team for the 1952 Monte Carlo Rally.

Moss was still a relative newcomer then, so we should not credit Garrad too highly for signing the best post-Nuvolari driver in the world. In fact, Moss sold himself. Determined to enter the Monte, he visited the Motor Show in 1951 looking for the right car. Not unexpectedly he picked Sunbeam-Talbot. His manager, Ken Gregory, asked Rootes what Moss's services were worth. 'He got the stock reply,' recalled Lewis Garrad: 'They were worth nothing! Provided Stirling was good, he might get a works product to use. And he took it. He did the rally for the usual expenses, which I think at that time were about £4 a day—there was no retainer pay

A most difficult photograph to identify adequately because little of the boot mounted rally plate is visible. However, it's an interesting car. Air horn trumpets are mounted on the front near-side wing and there's a raised air scoop on the louvred bonnet. The boot features two Monza alloy filler caps and there's an external door handle.

Also impossible to be accurate with, this shot shows off an Alpine leading a Triumph TR2 (only 2 litres) possibly at Silverstone. The Alpine comes with many accessories popular in the 1950s—headlamp peaks for example

at all for any team drivers. Times have changed dramatically, but I think the fun's gone out of it nowadays. But I know that's the way it was. Father somehow talked them all into it, but he didn't do it with money.' Lord Rootes knew what he was about, running his competitions with a Scot.

The 1952 Alpine presented the stellar trio of Moss/Cutts, Hawthorn/Chipperton and Murray-Frame/Pearman with some of the toughest conditions in the history of the event. In addition to the always-treacherous Alpine routes, the French organizers had increased average speeds and added the rough and tumble Dolomites to the course, which claimed at least two other Mark IIs, driven by George Hartwell and Leslie Johnson. Another Garrad recruit, American John Fitch, was forced out with a broken hub bearing. Nancy Mitchell, a pioneer 'Garrad Angel', failed to finish when her front wheels collapsed within 60 miles of the finish.

But none of this affected the first-string team. During the third stage between Cortina and Menaggio via Austria, Moss's car lost part of its exhaust system. He stopped for repairs, losing 26 minutes. Incredibly, he managed to make it up and eventually finish tenth overall, right behind Murray-Frame and Hawthorn. How he did it will never be known except to Moss, his co-driver and the occasional countryman who watched them pass. It was the kind of driving of which only Moss was capable, best characterized by his 1955 Mille Miglia navigator Denis Jenkinson: 'He was uncanny.'

The Sunbeam-Talbot trio won three Coupes, the Manufacturers' team prize and the Marseilles and Provence A.C. Challenge Cup. They were first in class in the acceleration and braking tests, once again giving up as much as 800cc to the competition. It was a superb rally.

By 1952, of course, the drivers had help from a thoroughly professional competition department, and the cars were well prepared. The need for frontal ventilation was apparently acute, since many

The Rootes team of Sunbeam-Talbot 90s for the 1953 International RAC Rally of Great Britain—second to a trio of XK120s—and driven by Ronnie Adams, George Hartwell and Norman Garrad. MWK17, Adam's car, took second place overall

Repairing the puncture that cost Sheila van Damm the Ladies' Prize in the 1953 Monte Carlo Rally

cars used an extra bonnet scoop and intakes built into the front aprons, in addition to the stock Mark II intakes.

Garrad's interest in lady drivers was strongly evident by 1953, through the multi-Coupes des Dames-winning Nancy Mitchell, and through the performances of Sheila van Damm. 'Sheila had got a bad press because she was a van Damm and they thought she was a nightclub owner's daughter,' Lewis Garrad noted. 'They were mistaken. Sheila was a very brave girl. She would never lift her foot, and would keep going when others would give up. Nothing ever got her down. She had tremendous ability and character—and character is very important in a driver. Later she quit abruptly, but that was her decision, nobody else's. Her father was ill and had

wanted her to get more involved in the business. But while she was with us, she was superb.' Sheila's first race for Rootes was the 1952 *Daily Express* Rally, in which she finished third in the Ladies' Class without any prior coaching. Through 1953–55 she took several Coupes des Dames, and she bested the field during the acceleration and braking tests at the 1954 Alpine.

That name Alpine had become so intrinsically interwoven with Sunbeam that it was a logical choice for a new model—a sports two-seater, announced in 1953. Though it has been suggested that this car stemmed from Rootes' desire to cater to the Americans, its inspiration in fact was strictly domestic, through George Hartwell.

'Hartwell', Lewis Garrad recalled, 'was a very big man, over six-three, strong, with tremendous courage and very little sympathy towards the cars. He had very little sympathy towards anybody. He demanded and got complete and utter loyalty and devotion. If he wanted something done it had to be done. He took no criticism. He was as bad as my father!

'Aside from being a top rally driver, George was a big Rootes dealer in Bournemouth—completely independent, though his firm was taken over eventually. In 1952, he took a Sunbeam-Talbot drophead and modified it by cutting the bodywork, creating a two-seater body. He also fitted twin carburettors, and soon found out that with the extra torque, third gear would break like hell. George got very good at changing gearboxes.

'After he built this car he brought it up to Coventry, and B. B. Winter decided to build it. Here we had a really beautiful-looking car. It was, I think, ahead of its time. To use it for rallying took a lot of work, but we had the basics right—the suspension, steering and gearbox—eventually.'

There are mixed opinions about the origins of the Alpine two-seater's body design. One theory has it that the car closely followed Hartwell's ideas, with minimal input from Clare Hodgman and the Loewy Studios. Hodgman himself thinks the lines were set down by Mr Poppe, managing director of Thrupp & Maberly. Robert E.

Many privateers used the Sunbeam Talbot on British rallies in the 1950s. This one's a 90 on the 1954 Margate Rally. Looks to be doing but a steady 30mph here, however!

TENTATIVE DE RECORDS. Marque de véhicule: Sunbeam-Talbot. Catégorie / Classe

Stirling Moss. Moteur de 4 cylindres Alésage 81.² mm Course 109.⁸ mm Cylindrée 2273

Jabbeke le 17-3-1953.

DÉPART LANCÉ — DÉPART ARRÊTÉ.

DISTANCES		ESSAI N° I (G à 0)	ESSAI N° II (0 vers G)	ESSAI N° III	ESSAI N° IV	ESSAI N° V	ESSAI N° VI	TEMPS MOYENS
1 KM.	Arrivée	10 13 47 05	10 23 25 23					I 18 73
	Départ	10 13 28 32	10 23 06 66					II 18 57
	TEMPS	18 73	18 57					18 65
	Vitesse à l'heure / km. par heure	192.205 / 119.430	193.861 / 120.459					193.029 / 119.942
1 Mile	Arrivée	10 13 50 55	10 23 25 23					I 30 23
	Départ	10 13 28 32	10 22 55 02					II 30 21
	TEMPS	30 23	30 21					30 22
	Vitesse à l'heure / km. par heure	191.651 / 119.086	191.778 / 119.165					191.714 / 119.126

Les commissaires SPORTIFS   Les commissaires TECHNIQUES.   Les CHRONOMÉTREURS

Proof of the performance—
Stirling Moss's specially-
prepared Sunbeam Alpine
achieved a best speed of
120.459mph on the Jabbeke
road, in Belgium, in 1953

Bourke, however, thinks the car was designed—or at least finalized
—back at Loewy's headquarters in South Bend. He has an amusing
tale to tell about it:

'As I recall, we built a small-scale clay model of this car in South
Bend. One of those involved was a young stylist named Kurt
Boehm. Kurt and I were then told that the model had to be in New
York within 24 hours. We grabbed a bullet-nosed Studebaker
convertible and headed for New York, driving flat-out across
Indiana, Ohio and Pennsylvania.

'We took some beer along for company, and I regret to say that
about halfway Kurt got sick. He leaned outside, but we had the
top down and the wind blew a lot of it back—all over the model.
We got to New York in a panic. Mr Loewy was to show it to the
Rootes people the next morning. We'd washed it down with beer
when the accident happened, but that didn't help, so we went out
and bought cheap perfume and sloshed it all over the model.'

Next morning the hard-used Sunbeam Alpine clay model was
duly handed over to Raymond Loewy, who walked around it,
looking at it from every angle and, as was his wont, getting quite
close to observe detail. 'Eet looks very fine, Bob,' Loewy said in his
on-off French accent, 'but eet smells a leetle funnee, no?' Said
Bourke, 'I never sweat so hard in my life. Anyway, we managed to
go through with the presentation and, as far as I know, Rootes were
delighted.'

Clare Hodgman suggests the Alpine's rationale: 'I think Sir
William Rootes felt that in the line they were missing the sports car
category. I remember being shown a little clay model resembling
the early Fiat 500s when the work was just getting started. What

Not everyone could afford to, or even wanted to, forget the 90 for competition in the mid-fifties. This drophead of 1954 vintage is competing on the 1954 BARC Eastbourne Rally. The then Mark IIA had only a few horsepower less than the two seater Alpine

we ended with was something closely related in frontal aspect to the 90, different only in its louvred bonnet. From the cowl back, it had a separate character of its own.'

The Thrupp & Maberly clay model must have been an alternative prepared by that Rootes subsidiary, since the Alpine bore no resemblance to the concurrent Fiat 500s. The design of Hartwell's car was very closely followed, except that the final product had a longer double row of louvres. Grafted to the familiar front end was a smoothly rounded torpedo tail, which ran back from the twin bucket seats to taper down to the rear bumper. Like other Sunbeam-Talbots, the Alpine was luxuriously finished inside, with provision for all instruments, including a central rev counter, and the traditional column shift.

Mechanically, evolutionary changes were made to improve the performance. Compared to the concurrent Mark IIA, the Alpine had fractionally lower compression but higher horsepower: 80bhp at 4200rpm. The increase was accomplished by shortening valve guides and modifying the ports. Instead of Hartwell's twin carburettors, a single Stromberg DAA36 instrument was fitted. Maximum speed of the first models was 95mph. (Stirling Moss recently told Graham Robson, 'You wouldn't believe how slow my Sunbeams were.' Graham, having seen the specifications, said he would.) Overdrive became standard from autumn 1954, and the gear ratios were at this time widened. Overdrive Alpines could just exceed the ton, giving about 24mph per 1000rpm. Other mechanical changes included a Burgess straight-through silencer, Lucas sports coil with manual control, deeper radiator block, stiffer than standard springs and shock absorbers and larger anti-roll bar.

It was traditional at that time for sporting cars to prove themselves on the smidgen of motorway built near the town of Jabbeke in Belgium. An early Alpine (MWK 969) was duly fitted up for Sheila van Damm. It had a metal undershield and tonneau cover, and a fared driver's cowling in lieu of a windscreen. With this equipage and a razor-tune, van Damm managed 120.125mph for the flying kilometre. Leslie Johnson later drove the car at 121.2mph

One of the 1955 Monte
Carlo 'works' Mark III 90
saloons. Rootes were
triumphant on that occasion.
Per Malling won the event
and Sheila van Damm the
Coupe des Dames. This
looks like the van Damm car

at Montlhèry and Moss clocked 116mph at the same venue. These performances were not quite on par with the contemporary 2-litre Triumph TR2, which Ken Richardson drove to 125mph on the same stretch of highway, though 120 was good enough for a spate of publicity. In the long run, however, both the TR2 and Austin-Healey 100 BN1 proved far better sellers than the Alpine; they were both cheaper and quicker, though far less luxurious. Slow sales (by autumn 1953 only 13 had been sold in the USA) resulted in a decision to kill the model before its time, in 1955. The sedans and convertibles, known from 1954 as the Sunbeam Mark III, carried on through 1957.

Despite its short tenure, the Alpine proved itself a thoroughbred. Garrad entered six cars in the 1953 Alpine Rally and four drivers— Moss, Frame, van Damm and Fitch—won Coupes des Alpes. Moss looked 'polished and unhurried' on the Monaco driving tests as he nailed down sixth place overall while giving away 600 to 1200cc to three of the five cars ahead of him. The greatest disappointment was Sheila van Damm's; she lost two minutes fixing a puncture and with it the Ladies' Prize. But the Alpine proved itself. 'There is no doubt of the ability of Sunbeam-Talbots to respond to a rally's demands,' wrote *The Autocar*.

Nineteen fifty-four was a bittersweet year—more rally wins, more sales losses. Moss drove a S-T 90 Mark IIA saloon this year, contributed to the team prize win at the Monte and gathered himself a Coupe des Alpes in the Alpine Rally. The ironies were yet more poignant in 1955. In the Monte Carlo Rally, Sunbeam recorded its first outright win—with a private entry owned and driven by a Norwegian.

The 1955 Monte was a reversal of tradition. Instead of the usually rotten southern conditions, bad weather plagued starters from the north—Glasgow, Munich, Oslo and Stockholm. Norway's Per Malling, starting from Oslo with his Mark III, encountered horrific snow in Denmark and Holland, yet arrived in Monte Carlo third overall behind a Citroën and a DKW. Malling did extremely well in the mountain tests, and gingerly nipped through the circuit competition with an ailing generator. 'He was determined to be careful, and the distinctly rough engine put him well back in the group,' *The Autocar* reported. (In fact he scored poorest among the top 20 finishers.) 'Although he was lapped by the Aston Martin of the Monegasque J. Mariage he finished the course— jubilantly.' Malling had made up for his circuit performance by besting everyone except Marang's Citroën on the regular course, and Marang had done so poorly in the mountain test that he finished tenth. The DKW virtually disappeared, and Malling was the winner. Sheila van Damm won the Coupes des Dames.

In eight brief years Norman Garrad had created a legend out of the barest raw ingredients, and they have been preserved—many of the cars in reality, all of the years in memory. Those memories are full ones, and there are still many who recall the Sunbeam-

Talbots boring down straights lined with spectators, charging up hills only to smoke brakes down the other side, skimming precipices at speeds no earthly mortal had any right to be travelling. They may remember too the humorous moments: of Norman Garrad checking the air flow from an Alpine's bonnet louvres with a feather duster, finding it inadequate and drilling extractor holes in the sides; of hefty Sheila van Damm committing near-permanent damage to herself lifting the corner of a car to assist a tyre change in lieu of a working jack. They were great days.

The old styling had become quite long in the tooth by 1957, and the sales figures were reflecting this. New designs were already in the field, and with them a new rally effort. But in those now fast-obsoleting lines was the shape of a thoroughbred. Today's owners of Sunbeam-Talbot 90s and Alpines may be justly proud, for they are motoring in a retired champion, as worhy of respect in its own milieu as a Joe Louis or a Stirling Moss. Such cars are artifacts of a time when rallying was somehow fiercer, freer, cheaper and more fun. Long may they be remembered.

Stirling Moss's Alpine being prepared for the subsequently cancelled Alpine Rally of 1955 (after the Le Mans disaster). On the left is Norman Garrad, then to his left John Cutts and on the other side of the car, mechanic Gerry Spencer

4

From dowager to thoroughbred

The Sunbeam Rapier, as it appeared on the floor of Earls Court in October 1955, was nothing to write home about. *Motor Sport*'s William Boddy called it 'more of a "hotted-up" Hillman Minx than a Gran Turismo or sports saloon,' a correct if somewhat delimiting description. The Rapier was never blessed with high style; it had to survive with the dowdy but serviceable Minx design, albeit in pillarless form, and vivid two-tone paint jobs like red/grey or yellow/white, which were highly controversial. In the Sunbeam line the Rapier initially lived in the shadow of the more esoteric Mark III; later it was eclipsed by the 'new' Alpine and the Tiger. Yet the Rapier won itself a devoted clientele—and more than its share of rallies. From an ill-handling little beast in 1955, it evolved into a formidable competitor in just four years.

Documenting Rapier history requires a look at the marketing goals of Sir William Rootes, in particular his fascination with the North American market. As champion of dollar exports he was unmatched and indefatigable. When Britain was still commanding a 40 per cent share of the US import market, Rootes was telling the industry this was 'not nearly sufficient', that more modern methods and products were necessary to maintain that standing. Who, in the light of retrospect, could say he was wrong?

Sir William took an early jump on this market by establishing Rootes Motors Inc., with offices at 505 Park Avenue, New York City, in April 1950. Two months later he declared to the Royal Society of Arts, 'We must have broad highways,' suggesting that the way to sell cars to the Americans was to duplicate their standards of style and luxury with British-size cars—luxury compacts, in modern parlance.

Now this sort of talk was a mite controversial, and in fact such attitudes were considered heresy by a lot of entrenched thinkers in Coventry. American cars of the fifties tended to be garish, vulgar and overbodied. Many Britons thought the way to sell the US market was to offer alternatives, like the 'Auntie' Rover—the very antithesis of a tailfinned Cadillac Eldorado. Sir William argued that Britain could never move many of those things across the pond,

Peter Harper behind the wheel with Sheila van Damm waving, pretending to be doing some timed standing starts. This is an early Rapier, in 1956, still in its Hillman Minx lookalike bodyshell. Detail design of this car closely follows that of the 1953 Studebaker

What's not clear from this shot of the Mark I Rapier is where the paints actually change colour. It could be along that wavy line underneath the running strip. This may be the first production run model in early 1955

yet it *could* adapt snazzy interiors and two-tone paint jobs to the smaller cars it was already building at home, and attract Americans who wanted good performance coupled with style and economy—qualities not available in one package from Detroit.

Coupled to Sir William's drive for broader markets—he emphasized the Commonwealth equally with the United States—was vast expansion of the Rootes Group throughout the fifties. In 1951, they took over the commercial vehicle/motor bus builders Tilling-Stevens of Maidstone, and in late 1955 Rootes absorbed Singer. Sir William thus came full circle, for he had begun his industry career as a Singer trade apprentice. Now he was Singer chairman.

Singer of Birmingham had once ranked just behind Austin and Morris among British car manufacturers, but had fallen upon hard times. With a dwindling postwar market share, they were never able to afford a replacement for the obsolete SM1500, and their rather novel twin-cam 1955 engine was too little, too late. Rootes stepped in with an offer of just £235,000 and a shares issue, acquiring Singer's gross assets of over £2 million, including the factories at Birmingham and Coventry. The Birmingham factory ultimately became Rootes' huge spares department, while the Coventry establishment evolved to a component supply centre for Ryton. The Rootes' Singers emerged as badge-engineered off-shoots of the Hillmans, initially with the Singer engines, but by 1959 with standard Hillman power. The Singer acquisition broadened Rootes' 'divisional' concept of marketing, making the Group a sort of mini-General Motors, bracketing numerous markets with just two or three basic specifications. Hillman served the basic transport need; Singer provided a little luxury; Humber was the top of the line; and Sunbeam was 'sporty'. The stage was set for the Sunbeam Rapier.

The aforementioned Mr Boddy was the only motoring journalist to report on the *raison d'être* of the new Rapier, which was introduced at Earls Court in October 1955, and his remarks, from the April 1956 *Motor Sport*, are interesting: 'The competition was that of an all-round high-performance car, possessing a more general appeal than its famous predecessor, the Mark III Sunbeam, which is, perhaps, a car primarily for the enthusiast. [Through early 1957 the Mark III was still in production.] It was felt that a

The 'old' Hillman Minx 1390 engine was slightly revised for the first Rapier to give just 62 horsepower. Nothing too startling, though

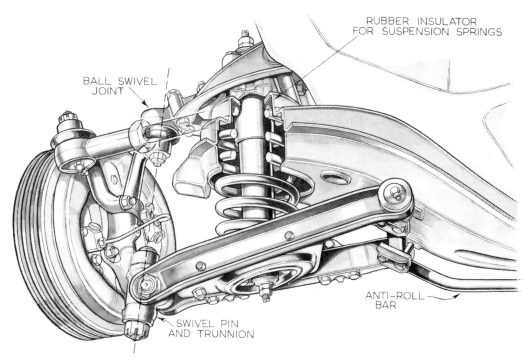

RUBBER INSULATOR
FOR SUSPENSION SPRINGS

BALL SWIVEL
JOINT

ANTI-ROLL
BAR

SWIVEL PIN
AND TRUNNION

small compact five-seater saloon, outstanding in respect of speed and acceleration allied to good fuel consumption, easy on the eye and of modern appearance, would admirably meet the needs of world markets. A stylist of international repute planned the body lines. . . .'

Who the stylist of international repute was, *Motor Sport* did not say, but the reader may be able to guess. Boddy was referring to Raymond Loewy—or more exactly the Loewy Studios—represented in London by Clare Hodgman. And Rapier styling was closely related to the contemporary Loewy-styled Studebakers.

The Rapier had been under development for about two years prior to introduction, which places its design around 1953. This year is remembered in Stateside circles as the time when Studebaker introduced its Loewy-designed Starliner and Starlight coupés—the outstanding American design of the decade. Low and lithe, these graceful creations of Loewy's chief designer Robert E. Bourke received international acclaim, and one of the acclaimants was Sir William Rootes.

Detail design of the Mark I Rapier is clearly related to the 1953 Studebaker. I emphasize the word detail, for the cars were not related in basic bodyshells or chassis-drivetrains. Consider, however, the numerous touches that the first Rapier shared with the Studebaker Starliner hardtops: the shape of the roof, particularly the rear pillars; the concave moulding along the body sides; the chrome-rimmed headlamps. There is no doubt that Loewy's people had a hand in both cars.

Solid conventional independent front suspension, as used on the Sunbeam Rapier of 1955, which was later given disc brakes, and was adapted to smaller, 13 inch road wheels

Privateers often found the Rapier a suitable vehicle for competition, particularly in its early days. This is Major H. G. Baldwin at Stapleford Airfield in May of 1958. This venue was one for the National Speed Hill Climb Championship of that year. This car has the 67.5bhp engine

Another hillclimb venue was used during the RAC Rally of 1958; this is Prescott for this Series II Rapier, the first of its own identity. Apart from the lack of wheel trims and two extra driving lamps the car looks pretty standard

By 1958 and the arrival of the Series II Rapier the factory was pretty serious about rallying. This car is typical of the Monte preparation of the day—driving lamps with Perspex protective covers (same for the headlamps, but less obvious) and the big across-bonnet windscreen 'cleaner'. Car was painted in Rootes strange mid-grey and deep-red two-tone

The resemblance is heightened when considering the 1958 Series II Rapier, with its upright grille and tailfins. This model was designed for Rootes in 1955—at the same time Loewy Studios were creating the 1956 line of Studebaker Hawks. The 1958 Rapier and 1956 Hawks share many features: upright grilles, small flanking grilles (a feature Sunbeam may have inspired for Studebaker), concave tailfins, upright tail-lamps at the tips of the rear wings. Both interiors were richly and colourfully upholstered and both were equipped with a full complement of instruments. Did one influence the other? I asked Bob Bourke, then Loewy's chief designer, who replied, 'Oh yes, certainly. These were little details we had tried and liked on one or the other car, and it was only natural that they spill over.'

One spillover which Sir William didn't care for at all was Studebaker's use of the word 'Hawk'—a Humber model name since 1945. In December 1955 he wrote to a friend at Studebaker: 'We have seen your [adverts] and are flattered that the name HAWK appears so prominently. The only mistake you have made, is that you have added the word STUDEBAKER instead of HUMBER . . . we have used the word HAWK very extensively throughout the world . . . What is more, it is registered as a trademark in the USA, Canada and elsewhere in the world. Obviously the Rootes family do not wish to create difficulties over this, but we would be interested to know what you and your colleagues suggest.'

20th International Alpine Rally, 23 to 30 June, 1959. Here at Cannes after the event are (left) Les Leston and Peter Jopp and (right) Paddy Hopkirk and Jack Scott—they came third overall. Scoops for getting air in and out and side exhausts are of note

Not exhibited on the Autobianchi stand at the Paris Show in 1959 was the Series II Rapier Convertible. It had all that was necessary to win over a number of loyal customers. Today, few are extant because of the ravages of rust

Gorgeous girls are usually used to divert attention from nasty cars, but in the case of the Rapier there was surely no need. . . . Daring stuff in the 1950s

Studebaker-Packard counsel Alfred E. Wilson wrote a careful reply, stressing that the word 'hawk' (he used lower-case) would 'always be used, not only in association with the name Studebaker but also in association with other words to designate particular characteristics'. (The 1956 models were the Golden, Sky, Flight and Power Hawks.) These were, Wilson said, 'compound names', and evidently his argument satisfied Rootes. But in 1960, Studebaker-Packard reversed itself, applying the Hawk title without any modifying word. Rootes protested again, and by 1962 Studebaker changed the designation to 'Gran Turismo Hawk'. The Humber Hawk continued in production through 1967, while the Studebaker version vanished after 1964.

Motive power for the new Rapier was a tuned version of the Hillman Minx 1390cc engine, the first Rootes powerplant built without reference to the old RAC horsepower rating, which was based on piston area, i.e. bore but not stroke. Its bore and stroke were exactly even at 76.2×76.2mm, and the Rapier developed 62.5bhp at 5000rpm, some 15bhp more than the Minx engine. This was a relaxed state of tune, for the 1390 had been designed with such improvements in mind. It had oversized bearings, a large-capacity oil pump and a stiff crankshaft and connecting rods. The power gain over the Minx was provided through 8:1 compression and a Stromberg 36 DIF carburettor. Torque was 73.2lb ft at 3000rpm. To cope with the added urge, the Rapier clutch was of 8in diameter, instead of 7.25in as on the Hillman.

In body construction the Rapier followed the path laid down by Hillman, and very specifically the Minx Californian, Britain's first volume saloon of over 1-litre capacity with two instead of four doors. The British market was not attuned to the idea of two-door saloons, but what Americans called the 'hardtop convertible' had come of age across the pond, and was enjoying a 30 per cent share of sales there. Since the Rapier was primarily sporting transportation, the loss of two doors was not considered crucial. But the decision undoubtedly contributed to fairly modest sales in England.

Two-door construction did permit the use of stiff bodywork without adding weight, since the rear door cutaways were unnecessary. Pillarless roof construction, probably inspired by the Loewy Studebaker, allowed an unbroken expanse of open air at each side of the car, which was also a novelty.

Unit construction of body and chassis wasn't unique to the Rootes Group, and had strong advantages—great strength per unit weight and economies of production. Already the method had been espoused by Nash and Hudson in the US, and Austin, Morris and Standard in the UK. Like Hudson's, the Rapier floorline was of the 'step-down' variety, lower than the body sills. This allowed a lower roof without sacrificing legroom, though the roofline seemed high even at that.

Unit construction also meant that Rootes could alter its usual method of carrying the main body load with two longitudinal frame rails. In the Rapier's case the weight was carried by hefty cross-members tied into the body sills and stiffened by the floor and propshaft tunnel structure. The front member was just behind the overdrive casing, while the rear member was at the leading anchor points of the rear springs. The unit body allowed even distribution of weight throughout the structure and provided a significant improvement in torsional strength—qualities which proved useful on the rally circuits.

The Series III Rapier saw the good basics refined further. Major visual difference is the shape of the side strips, now no longer over the rear fins. Wheels are still thin, diameters large and tyres cross-ply. Hard to forget it's only 1960

This Series IIIA Rapier facia was typical of those fitted to the 'classic' Rapiers of the 1960s. The overdrive, when fitted, was operated by a switch mounted on the steering column.

The 'works' continued to conduct a stiff rally programme for the cars. Externally the cars hadn't changed much since the Series II. Unusual to have three members of the crew for the Monte Carlo. It's 1961

One of the famous 'YWK' team cars—Mark III Rapiers—at the start of the 1961 Monte Carlo Rally. Left to right is Mike Parkes, Peter Wilson, Gregor Grant, Peter Harper, Raymond Baxter and Peter Procter

In keeping with contemporary trends, the Rapier used ifs via long and short wishbones. This was mounted on a box-section subassembly bolted to the chassis at eight points. Rubber-insulated coil springs encircled rubber-mounted telescopic dampers. The live rear axle was semi-floating, supported by semi-elliptic leaf springs. An extra leaf on the bottom of each spring became effective at higher wheel deflections—in effect creating a variable spring rate. Rear shock absorbers, also telescopic, were mounted in a near-vertical position, allowing the full piston stroke to be utilized against loads. Steering was by Burman worm and nut mounted on the body frame members level with the rear of the cylinder block. The driver faced a two-spoke sprung steering wheel with semi-circular horn ring, and 2.5 turns were required lock-to-lock.

Off-the-shelf components were important in keeping the price of the Rapier down (even so, it cost £1044 including purchase tax, against only £780 for the Californian). Thus Rootes used a Hillman engine and a Rootes gearbox with synchromesh on the top three ratios. Specially developed by Laycock for the Rapier was a new, smaller overdrive unit operating on the top three gears controlled by a flick switch in the centre of the facia. The gear selector remained on the column as in earlier Sunbeams.

Much of the added cost over a Californian was concentrated in the Rapier's interior, a studied contrast with comparable cars of its day. A large speedometer and rev counter squarely faced the driver, and four auxiliary gauges were mounted at the top centre, plainly in view. Miscellaneous switches, an optional clock and controls for the optional radio and heater were carried in a central console, flanked by a package shelf on the driver's side and a lockable cubby in front of the passenger. The duotoned upholstery used pleated leather for seat facings, and came with colour-keyed carpeting. The impression was one of Detroitish luxury, with many a piece of traditional walnut to be seen.

The exterior, too, gave little evidence of British origins, comprising what the editor of *Motor Sport* diffidently called 'the Gay-Look'. It is interesting that the same gentleman called the Rapier 'attractively-compact', its two-tone paintwork 'nicely offset by the chromium-ringed, hooded in-built headlamps', because such a confection, in theory, had been heartily condemned in the self-same issue. One way or the other, American influence on this car was very strong.

More interesting were Boddy's comments on his test Rapiers after some 700 miles' experience during the summer of 1956. He found the engine lively but noisy, and the steering column change 'no better than most of its type'. The overdrive worked well, but a considerable ratio gap (5.22 to 3.95) was engineered into the top gears. Thus 'an average driver selecting overdrive [causes] considerable load on the back axle and a jerk which passengers with sensitive stomachs seem to find unpleasant, or even disastrous. . . .' The overdrive did provide a useful extension of the upper gears: direct third and top yielded only about 50 and 80mph, while their overdrive counterparts gave 70 and 85mph. But the ratios should have been better chosen, for overdrive third was almost the same as direct top. Further, first gear was ultra-low, and reserved for 'emergency starting'. The owner's manual actually warned that it 'should be engaged occasionally to prevent it becoming stiff from disuse'!

The Mark IIIA Rapier came in Convertible form too. Much as before except for the 1600cc engine and its 80bhp

Another familiar shot from the Rootes publicity department. This is the Mark IIIA 1592cc engine and gearbox with Solex compound carburettor. The standard Rapier engine was never highly tuned although on paper, at least, it could have produced more power. The cars were heavy

Motor Sport found the Rapier predictable in the dry, mildly understeering, with final oversteer setting in on a tight corner. In the wet, though, 'the wheels lose adhesion rather early and the safety factor becomes open to question'. The steering was found to lack feel and the suspension to be rather soft. The 9in Lockheed 2LS brakes were 'none too convincing', though the handbrake, mounted Rootes-fashion outboard of the driver's seat, was said to be 'very sensible'. Boddy concluded that his test Rapiers were 'both pleasing and disappointing'. He had serious reservations about their handling which, he suggested, 'may be a contributory cause of three works Rapiers coming to disaster in this year's Alpine Rally (in which, however, one of these cars won the 'standard' 1600cc category). . . .' We should thus turn to the Rapier's first experience in competition, to learn what happened.

The original Rapier was considered by most in the competitions department to be a pretty ordinary car compared to the S-T 90. The first time the Garrads looked at it they remember saying, 'Forget it, pack the bags and let's go home.' But it was the latest product, and it needed all the competition success they could wring out of it. Away they went. . . .

The initial effort was the 1956 Mille Miglia, where two cars ran: a works entry for Peter Harper/Sheila van Damm, and a private Rapier driven by Wisnewski/Bosmiller. Both finished the 1000 miles in 15.5 hours, a 65mph average—in company with many faster cars. This gave the Rapier a 1–2 finish in the 1600cc Special Touring class. In the Tulip Rally, four cars were entered and all

Workshop preparations for the 1962 Monte Carlo Rally—with Jim Ashworth and Norman Garrad looking over Ernie Beck's engine bay work in the ex-Le Mans Sunbeam Alpine

finished in the top ten. Private entrant John Melvin was the class winner.

For the always-challenging Alpine Rally, some 'cheats' were tried—aluminium panels and bumpers. This ploy was caught by the organizers—who were not fools—but the team was allowed 12 hours to set the cars right. 'And quite honestly the basic weight was in the chassis,' Lewis said. 'You could only save a few pounds in the doors and bumpers.'

Sadly, the Alpine Rally was a disaster. Though two of the five Sunbeam Rapiers finished (Harper/Humphrey twenty-third and Deane/Sparrow twenty-eighth), the other three met with serious accidents. George Murray-Frame, who had been going splendidly, collided with a Porsche; Raymond Baxter, seemingly very fast in the rain, finally crashed at Mégève and Jim Ryan went 'over the edge' at the Vivione Pass.

One significant event of the 1956 season was the maiden performance of a rally driver whose name was to become synonymous with Sunbeam, Peter Harper. Born in 1921, Harper had entered rallying with a Sunbeam-Talbot 2-litre in 1947, staying with the marque as a private driver through 1956, when he joined Garrad's team. Despite what was evidently unperfected machinery in the original Rapier, Harper won his class in the Mille Miglia and had the top Rapier in the Alpine.

'Peter Harper came up through the ranks because he was a starter on his own,' Lewis Garrad recalled. 'He'd come up through the Talbot Owners' Club. Some of their drivers were *prime donne*, who knew as much about engineering as from A to B. But Peter

The ever-glamorous Rosemary Smith (left), who was not only decorative but also won many many Ladies' Prizes for Rootes in the 1960s

Hard a port! And just *look* at the tyre distortion on Tiny Lewis's Rapier IIIA team car, at Station Hairpin on the Monaco GP circuit, during the final tests of the 1962 Monte Carlo Rally

had an understanding of the problems of a rather big manufacturer. He knew why we couldn't do major development work, and was very aware of the marketing advantage of being out on the market with this type of car. And, of course, he used his work to his advantage in his Rootes dealership. He would promote and sell the cars.' Harper would continue to race Rapiers into the early sixties—and usually with distinction.

The first modification to the Rapier occurred in September 1956, when the R67 engine arrived, unchanged in dimensions, but producing 67.5bhp at 5400rpm via twin Zenith carburettors. This gave slightly better acceleration, but added nothing to the top speed. It was not enough, and the only successes of 1957 were a Jimmy Ray/Ian Hall class win in the Tulip Rally and a second-in-class at the Mille Miglia. After 1957, however, things began to change dramatically.

'Engineering at that time had a lot more of the younger element in it,' Lewis Garrad continued, 'and even the more mature engineers who lived with them through that period had some of their enthusiasm rub off. They all had decided that they wanted this car to be a winner. Engineering certainly worked damn hard on that car, and they did a lot of work.' The Series II Rapier, introduced for the 1958 model year, was a strong improvement on what had gone before, and evidence that the engineers had paid heed to rally competition experience.

The Appendix to this book details the changes in engine specification, though this—as important as it was—was not the key to the improvement. Briefly, a bore increase brought capacity up to 1494cc; with increased compression this translated to 73bhp at 5200rpm and a useful 10 per cent increase in torque. The clumsy column gearchange finally gave way to a remote control lever sprouting properly from the floor, whilst overdrive—hitherto standard and operative on the top three gears—became a £63 option and worked on third and top only. (The rally team nevertheless managed to doctor it to work on second.)

More important to the rally team were the Series II's suspension and steering alterations, developed after much experimentation following the mixed performances of 1956–57. To improve roadholding, the diameter of the coil springs was increased by 0.03in and the spring rate from 305 to 370lb. A front anti-roll bar was fitted, along with Armstrong AT9 shock absorbers. To eliminate the Series I's heavy, imprecise steering, Rootes switched Burman steering set-ups: instead of the worm-and-nut P-type they adopted the recirculatory ball F-type. The steering ratio remained unchanged, but was lighter and far more positive. Incidental but useful alterations included a new angle of engine and gearbox mountings, which provided better insulation and less noise.

Designwise the Series II was a definite step ahead. The Series I's gaudy duotone panel was gone, though its shape remained (and always would remain) on the front wings. In its place was a slim strip painted the same colour as the roof. The rear wings now sprouted modest little fins, Studebaker's influence showing up

Rosemary Smith (at the wheel), Rosemary Seers and the 'team' Rapier IIIA, before the start of the 1963 Monte Carlo Rally

Rosemary Smith hurling her 'works' Rapier IIIA round a fast, open hairpin in the French Alps. By this time, in the early 1960s, the Rapier was an extremely competitive rally car

David Pollard (standing) and Tony Baines, making final adjustments to one of the last batch of 'works' rally Rapiers built, before starting the RAC International Rally. Note the sump shield. to protect the engine from rough surfaces

again. Up front, headlamp rims were painted in the body colours, and there was new dental work: a traditional squared-off grille flanked by two lower grilles, in the manner of the S-T 90s.

Significant from the sales standpoint was a second model, a three-position convertible. Like other Rootes dropheads it offered a middle 'coupe de Ville' position: the forward part of the hood folded back around a hefty cast steel hoop, which was held in posi-

Alan Fraser not only ran racing Rapiers, but found time to go rallying himself. Here he is, in one of his own cars, ready to tackle a Monte of the early 1960s

tion by a positive locking device controlled by knurled knobs. It was a unique arrangement, harking back to motoring past, though the knobs were inviting things for passengers to play with. The soft-top Rapier listed for £1104 with Purchase Tax, only £60 more than the hardtop. Overdrive cost £63 extra.

The added power of what Rootes-USA called the 'Rally-master' engine showed up in some road tests. On average, the Series II was about 2.5 seconds quicker, achieving 60mph, and had close to 90mph available. The '58s' were, of course, higher geared; rear axle ratios of both the overdrive (4.78) and standard (4.55) models were much altered from the Series I's 5.22 ratio. The mph/1000rpm figure in top was now 16.06, compared to 14.0 in the Series I; in overdrive it was 20.23 against 18.5. Lack of an overdrive second did create a gap in the ratios. Yet overall it was a worthy new generation, and Garrad's rallymen got happily to work. Peter Harper started the ball rolling by teaming with Bill Deane to win the 1958 RAC Rally outright.

This event was planned to be rugged, with 20 high-speed hill-climbing and manoeuvrability tests *en route*; the weather made it even rougher. This writer has driven Hard Knott Pass in the Lake District, and not slowly; but he can only begin to imagine what it must have been like in the snow and ice that March, when only 15 of the 196 cars managed the ascent. Battling a determined team of Standard Pennants and Tens, Harper/Deane drove a near flawless rally, finishing despite all travail without a dent. Standard won the Team Prize, but overall it was no contest: the Rapier had lost only 652.8 marks, against the second place Gouldbourn/Turner Pennant's 1179.3.

This performance was no fluke, for Rapiers continued to find success: they were first and second in the 1300–1600cc class at the Circuit of Ireland, winners of the Team Prize at the Tulip Rally, outright and class winners at Uganda's Mount Elgon Rally and outright winners (with only 5 marks lost) of the London Rally. The performance of the season was the Alpine Rally, at which Rapier IIs finished 1-2-3-4-5 in class, won the Coupes des Alpes and were third in the Coupe des Dames.

The Alpine threw all its notorious horrors at competitors that year, routing cars through treacherous Alps, and then, after driving tests at Monza over the gravelled Dolomites, back across Stelvio Pass, on to Milan via the Vivione and into France via Mégève, Grenoble and Gap, then to Marseilles by a roundabout route across the Cayolle, the Allos and Mont Ventoux. It was Harper starring once again, teamed with Peter Jopp: their Rapier was sixth overall and the class winner.

'There is no doubt', wrote Michael Frostick, 'that by this time the Rootes competition department had really got to grips with the regulations and those little bits of knowledge which make all the difference to the running of the team in the event, and this, coupled with very careful preparation of the cars, which provided useful improvements in power output, was beginning to pay dividends.' Lewis Garrad adds: 'By this time there was a semblance of a design assistance team. We found that an engineer could come to us and say, "this is the thing we're thinking of; would you try this?" Okay, we'd do it. The regulations weren't as strict as they are today, and we'd run some pretty weird cars with different suspension settings. We didn't change the specifications, but we'd use different steering ratios, axle ratios. We'd bang around with suspensions, trying to shift things about, trying to make the suspensions last.

'Things were pretty loose until the regulations became structured. Everybody cheated, of course. I remember we'd take pictures of Citroën doing something illegal and they'd take pictures of us, and we each agreed not to tell, which I guess is when the system came into disrepute. After the structure tightened up it was much harder for cheaters. We concentrated hard on tyres, for example, because they wouldn't allow changes. You didn't have ice or snow tyres, or wet tyres, or anything except one set of dashed bloody tyres. And you lived with them.' But whatever the Rootes team were doing, they were doing right.

For 1959 the team gained perhaps the best-known rally driver in history, Ulsterman Paddy Hopkirk. Then 26, Hopkirk had had five years' driving experience under the Standard-Triumph banner. His high point of 1958 had been the Circuit of Ireland, which he'd won with a TR3. Hopkirk would remain with Rootes through 1962; he was very much an individualist, and didn't always agree with team management decisions. Remarkably, nobody on the Rootes team in these years was ever paid big money. 'We paid

A typical Rootes/Ford/BMC racing battle at Silverstone in 1963, with Peter Harper's Rapier being leaned on by Paddy Hopkirk's Mini-Cooper, and Alan Hutcheson's Riley 1.5 very close to Jimmy Blumer's Cortina Super

Peter Harper, and we paid Paddy Hopkirk a little, but it wasn't much,' Garrad says—'a couple of hundred pounds at best.' Was it that they just liked Rapiers?

Led by the trio of Harper, Jopp and Hopkirk, Sunbeam could do no wrong in 1959. A Rapier was fifth overall and 'best British' in the Monte, where all of them finished. In the Alpine, Hopkirk and Jack Scott won third, trailing only two high-performance GT cars, while Jopp/Leston were sixth. Ronnie Adams demonstrated the worth of his Rapier II by tearing away most of the offside sheet metal in a shunt, then tying the door closed and driving back to Cannes without further incident. Sunbeam won its class in the Liège-Rome-Liège Rally, a vicious event in which only 14 of 97 cars finished. The victory was posted by Jimmy Ray and Mike Cotton, who finished eleventh overall.

As the fifties passed momentously into the sixties, onetime garageman Billy Rootes found himself at his apogee. He had been appointed a Baron—an hereditary title. He owned a yacht and a palatial estate in Wiltshire. The Rootes family was in secure control of the company, whose destiny looked good. Rootes held a 10.6 per cent share of the UK market, following closely behind Vauxhall, though well behind BMC and Ford. In America, where the Hillman Minx and Husky still sold in appreciable numbers, Rootes had introduced the Humber Super Snipe (1958) and Singer Gazelle (1959); together with the Rapier and the newly introduced Sunbeam Alpine, the Group was averaging a respectable 4 per cent of the US import market, selling upwards of 20,000 cars per year.

Rapiers of this basic shape were in production from 1955 to 1967—this was a Series IV version, with 1592 cc engine and disc brakes, along with the smaller diameter, 13 in wheels

But it was the same old Billy Rootes who might descend on the engineers after a boardroom luncheon, or drop down to the production line to chat with the blokes, or twiddle with the latest Sunbeam prototype at Lindley. Lord Billy might be 65, but he had no intention of retiring. Possibly he should have. The sixties were not kind to the Rootes Group; from the height of prosperity the company was destined to plunge rapidly downhill, to emerge as only a shell of their former selves in the next decade. But we digress.

For 1960 the Rapier was designated Series III, and received its final significant styling alterations, though several more series were still to come. Body changes included a thinner side colour sweep which no longer intruded on the vestigal tailfins, and a deeper windscreen accommodated by a lower scuttle. Together, these changes made the Series III readily identifiable from its predecessors, and did much to improve visibility and styling. On the inside, luxury had arrived in the form of a polished dark walnut facia, which encompassed all the instruments; the lower central console continued to house optional clock, radio and heater controls, but was wood-grained to match the rest of the ensemble. Series III and later Rapiers featured full circle horn rings— annoying devices which mainly served to get in the way of the rev counter. Many Rapier (and Alpine) drivers including this writer learned that the ring could be removed, and with the help of fibre spacers the horn could be activated via the centre boss.

The Series III drivetrain was modified along Alpine lines, with twin Zenith carbs and an alloy head of higher (9.2:1) compression ratio. Valve design was modified, with inlet and exhaust ports rearranged, and there was a water-heated inlet manifold. Though the Rapier III lacked the Alpine's four-branch exhaust manifold, 'performance' carb settings and twin wire mesh air cleaners, it was rated at the same 78bhp as the two-seater. Rapier engines also used a four-bladed fan, while Alpine fans had six blades.

Laycock de Normanville overdrive, operating on third and top gears, was still a Rapier option, but the road speed per 1000rpm was actually a shade less than on the Series II: 15.3mph in direct top, 20.3 in overdrive. Gear ratio modifications had, however, usefully narrowed the gaps between second/third and third/top. Even more happily, disc front brakes were now standard—strong Lockheed units with two pads per disc and automatic wear adjustment.

It should be obvious that rallying really did improve the breed in the case of the Sunbeam Rapier. What had begun as a luxurious but ordinary little tourer had developed—well ahead of most cars in its class—into the definitive performance saloon of the sixties: disc brakes, tight suspension, close ratio gears controlled by a floor lever, a high state of tune. The transformation, underway with the Series II, was complete with the Series III—done in under four years. The entire character of the car had changed, and Rootes lost no time in proving it on the 1960 rally circuit.

After an undistinguished performance with Series IIs in the RAC Rally, the team prepared again for the Monte. Their new Series III cars bore the number plates YWK 1 through YWK 5. Peter Harper, accompanied by the BBC's Raymond Baxter in YWK 5, was absolutely splendid in the Monte. The Germans had entered several works and works-backed Mercedes 220SEs, which were indomitable 1-2-3-5 finishers; but Harper was fourth, and Sunbeam was 'best British' for the third year running. Incredibly, Harper had navigated as well as driven part of the way—Baxter had become ill—and he did so with highly suspect timing instruments. This was also the year when the Harper/Proctor team came into its own for Sunbeam. The two won their class and the Acropolis Cup in the Acropolis Rally; they also won the 1300–1600cc class in the Alpine, followed by a flock of other Rapiers (in 2-3-5-6 positions). In California, the Rapiers were class champions in the International Compact Car Race at Riverside.

Of course it must be noted that these Rapiers were 'modified', in that they used many components from the Alpine sports car, which were homologated for the Rapier as well. Aside from a good product to begin with, success depended on careful preparation. A look at George Hartwell's schedule for a Series III Rapier may be of interest in this context.

Hartwell began with a standard engine built with magnafluxed, balanced parts. The cylinder head was polished and the valves ground in. Flexible petrol pipes were fitted between fuel pump and carb, waterproof plug covers installed, and the coil moved to a more accessible yet better-protected position on the wing valance. Strengthening work was done on the throttle linkage, engine bearer plate and dynamo bracket. A Mory radiator blind was fitted, along with Alpine-type wire mesh air cleaners. The gearbox was carefully tested part by part, and special attention was paid to the seals. Overdrive was modified to operate on second as well as third and top gears. The rear axle was inspected closely, then modified to

One of Alan Fraser's Rapiers in a touring car race at Silverstone. For a time the Fraser cars were effectively undercover 'works' machines

71

Most will be hard pushed to deferentiate between Mark IV and V Rapiers. 1964 Mark IV, this one, it's on 13 inch wheels but still cross-ply tyres and it has all-synchromesh transmission. The Mark V took the 'new' 1725 engine. Not many were made of either series

enable Weathermaster tyres with chains to be fitted and still clear the wing. Ferodo competition brake linings and a Clayton Dewandre Motorvac Servo Unit were bolted up. The entire chassis was checked at all weld and bolt points and strengthened where necessary. Armstrong shock absorbers with stiff settings were supplied, along with many other special components: a Helphos sign poster lamp, a 3in Perspex shield to better direct the demister, a laminated windscreen, lightweight driver's seat and fold-down hinges for the passenger seat-plus-headrest. Thermos bottle holders were placed on the lower B-post, a tool holder on the near-side front door, bonnet safety catches were fitted; the boot was fitted with a petrol can, a shovel and an Eversure hydraulic quick-lift jack. An Elopress tyre inflator was mounted next to the passenger seat. Tyres, mounted on selected wheels, were Dunlop Dura-bands for the Tulip, Alpine and British rallies, but Duraband spikes for the Monte Carlo. Thus, while there was nothing to render the works Rapiers in any way illegal, they were certainly a bit different than the ones that came off showroom floors.

Still riding the crest of success and able to afford a big push, Rootes and private entrants registered no fewer than 21 of the 110 British cars in the 1961 Monte Carlo Rally. The works fielded six Rapiers. Once again it was Harper leading the way to a 'best British' finish, winning his class and establishing the best lap of all at the Monaco GP circuit tests: 2:51.1, a time worthy of the best grand touring machines.

The Rapier's California triumph of 1960 saw the marque take up new challenges far from European borders, and in 1961 this effort spread to Mexico and East Africa. Pedro and Ricardo Rodriguez achieved a sensational 1-2 class win in Mexico's major race meeting, Ricardo returning the fastest lap at 69.9mph. No other make was even close.

The East African Safari, a noted car killer, was the scene of further Rapier thrusts in 1961. Attempting to better past performances, Rootes fielded many local drivers—this time—an advantage in the 3200-mile marathon pitting cars against incredible boulder-strewn tracks, herds of wandering zebra and the occasional enraged rhino, and native onlookers who might demonstrate their impatience with the whole business by hurling a spear or two at passing rallyists. J. P. Valumbia, a Tanganyika garage owner, teamed with I. M. Bakhsh and a Rapier to win Class C outright; a Humber Super Snipe driven by Canadian zoologist Lee Talbot finished fourth overall. Of 77 starters, only 38 came home.

Nineteen sixty-one represented the peak of Rapier success, and though the wins kept coming afterwards, they were fewer in number. The car itself continued through three more series. The Mark IIIA (1962–63) received a bored-out 1592cc engine and developed 80bhp. The Mark IV (1964–65) had a single Solex compound carb and developed only 78.5bhp; it also was the first Rapier with 13in instead of 15in wheels, although rally cars often appeared with the larger ones. For 1965, too, the Series IV had all-synchromesh transmission.

The final Series V (1966–67) received the strong five-main bearing 1725cc engine, and is perforce the most desirable Rapier of all for collectors. Aside from being the most durable powerplant yet, it was the most powerful. The Series V was capable of an honest 95mph, and could spring from rest to 60mph in 14 seconds.

Time waits for no one, of course, and by the mid-sixties the competition emphasis had shifted to the Sunbeam Alpine, followed by the Tiger, and eventually the Imp. Rapiers remained in the Rootes line-up, more as a nod to their proud heritage rather than to sales; certainly volume wasn't high for the Series IV and V, as good as they were. But the record stood and the record was a good one. From virtually nil in 1956, Rootes had built an automobile fully worthy to inherit the mantle, and extend the record, of the Sunbeam-Talbot 90.

Still the Mark IV, the interior was considered to be 'luxury' in its day (1965). Pillarless construction is obvious. Mark V took certain '1725 group' fittings

5

The Rootes Humbers: hardly bespoke?

In the 'collector car' world, Humber was a non-starter. Or at best a non-finisher. Those who include a Super Snipe, Pullman or Imperial in their stables are regarded as eccentrics—deviants. The big Rootes Humbers deserve better. The writer's experience is firsthand. While in no way sporting, Humbers are beautifully built with superb materials, and their engines are virtually bulletproof. There's still a place, as William Boddy wrote when testing one, for cars 'with interiors remindful of clubland'—burled walnut veneers and Connolly hides, West of England cloth and Wilton carpet', at least in my garage.

The first Humber motorcar appeared in 1898, an outgrowth of Thomas Humber's bicycle firm in Beeston, Notts. Humber cars were built both at Beeston and in Coventry until 1908, when the Coventry works took on the entire assignment.

Humber were successful competitors from the very beginnings of the motor industry. In 1903, for example, a 20hp Humber Four had the legs of the Coventry Daimlers at Phoenix Park, Castle-welland and Killorglin, Ireland. Humber 2.0-, 2.4- and 3.5-litre cars were class champions in the 1905 racing season. The 3.3-litre Beeston Humber of T. C. Pullinger and the Coventry Humber 3.3 of Louis Coatalen finished fifth and sixth respectively in the 1906 TT.

From 1912 on into the twenties, Fred Tuck's great competition Humbers were among the cars to beat at hillclimbs and at Brooklands. Lionel Martin, the big, bluff, ruddy-faced hillclimb and sprint driver, who built a generation of $1\frac{1}{2}$-litre Aston Martins, entered a 1.7-litre Humber in the 1933 Alpine Trial. He and Mrs Martin came home sixth in the 1501–2000cc class, bested only by Adlers, Alfas and a solitary Opel.

In the marketplace, of course, Humbers were aimed at the 'upward-mobile' owner who wanted a large and luxurious car, more exclusive than a mere jumbo Austin. Rootes, who acquired Humber in 1929, consistently focused on this goal. As late as 1950, for example, a Humber Super Snipe was the largest British luxury car one could buy for less than £1000. Humbers always represented good value for money.

Who else but Winston Churchill, with Field Marshal Montgomery in the front passenger seat, reviewing victorious troops from the rear of a Second World War Humber staff car

A showroom display at Devonshire House, with the patrician Humber Imperial behind a portrait of Britain's greatest political leader, Sir Winston Churchill

Through the thirties the Humber line grew more uniform. The four-cylinder cars disappeared after 1936, Rootes having taken the decision to leave their market to Hillman. By 1938 the entire Humber range had independent front suspension. Hydraulic brakes arrived on the 16 and 21hp models of 1939, which year also saw the first Super Snipe. Despite a model name that proved the butt of many a joke, the Super Snipe was a worthy car which extended Humber's reputation for value. It carried the big 4.1-litre six on a compact chassis, and it sold for under £400.

During the war, Humbers served His Majesty's forces with distinction, and impressed many a serviceman with their rugged, bulldog qualities under the worst possible conditions. Super Snipe

Not new (for this picture was taken in 1964), but still impressive, is this massive Humber Pullman, as used by the Coventry Corporation for many years. It dated from the late 1940s

tourers often accompanied Field Marshal Montgomery; the most famous of these, nicknamed 'Old Faithful', was preserved after the war and used on ceremonial occasions. Another Humber, which Monty called 'the Victory Car', took part in the invasion of Europe, and appeared in Army manoeuvres as late as 1951. Some Super Snipes were fitted with special wooden estate bodies; occasionally, their fabric roofs were peeled back to house bulky wireless equipment.

The Coventry works also produced specialized military vehicles, including 'ironside' saloons made of austenitic steel, which often carried members of the Royal Family or the Churchill cabinet. Sir Winston himself was photographed on inspection tours at home or abroad in open Humbers. Rugged four-wheel-drive Humbers were built as Army utility cars. Humber Pullman limousines, constructed by the Rootes' Thrupp & Maberly coachworks in London, were supplied to the US Army under what Churchill called 'reversed Lend-Lease'.

After the war, Humber revived its four-cylinder range by borrowing the 1944cc side-valve engine from the pre-war Hillman 14; also taken from Hillman was the model name 'Hawk'. This car shared its styling with the postwar Snipe and Super Snipe; its purpose was to offer Humber size and quality at a lower price. Through 1948, Hawks produced 56bhp at 3800rpm, with transverse leaf spring ifs and a live axle with semi-elliptical leaf springs at the rear. The Mark II of 1947–48 was the same package, except that its gearchange was moved from the floor to the steering column. This was no doubt influenced by American practice, and received mixed reviews in Britain. To Rootes credit, the column change was precise and easy to snick from gear to gear; the company stayed with it into the 1960s.

Just to prove that the Super Snipe of the late 1940s was capable of almost anything, Maurice Gatsonides drove one on the 1950 Monte Carlo rally into a remarkable second place overall, just 1.38 seconds in special test times behind the winning Hotchkiss sports saloon

In 1952, this Super Snipe was driven on the Monte Carlo Rally by Charles Eyre Maunsell (a Rootes dealer from Belfast)

Hustling large, long cars like the 1952 Humber Super Snipe through and up the mountain hairpins can't have been anyone's idea of fun. Look at the angles of the two offside wheels. The Sunbeam-Talbot 90 influence shows up well in this photograph (1952 RAC Rally)

The Mark III Humber Hawk, announced in October 1948 for the 1949 model year, was completely redesigned with help from the Loewy organization. Its status as an up-market Hillman was apparent, as the smooth, envelope body style was very close in design to the smaller Hillman Minx. Unlike the latter, however, Humber retained a separate chassis frame and the side-valve 1944cc engine. (Clare Hodgman later gave it a more 'important' vertical radiator grille.) The Hawk progressed through a Mark VI model from 1949 into 1957, adopting a more prominent grille with the Mark IV and Snipe-type flanking grilles with the Mark V.

Up market, the Humber range comprised both Snipe and Super Snipe, with 2.7 and 4.1-litre side-valve sixes repectively for the model years through 1948. These were pleasant-looking cars reminiscent of pre-war transatlantic styling practices. A standard, round-tail saloon and a more traditional, square-cut sports saloon were offered.

The postwar carriage trade saw both Pullman and Imperial models, the latter appearing with the Mark II Pullman in 1948. While Pullmans were outright limousines—with division windows to separate the chauffeur's compartment—Imperials were owner-driver cars, accommodating seven passengers and without a division window. The Pullman Mark III, and its stablemate the Imperial Mark II, were the last of this line, both being dropped after 1954.

While they lasted, these big Humbers won the approval of a distinguished clientele—all the way to the top. The Royal Appointment was earned by Humber after the company produced a string of cars for various Royal Tours. The first of these were two landaulettes by Thrupp and Maberly for the government of Southern Rhodesia. For the Royal Tour of Australia and New Zealand in 1948, Humber supplied no fewer than 24 cars: three landaulettes, two fully open touring cabriolets, ten Pullman limousines and nine Super Snipes.

The Pullman was the first big Humber to be restyled. Striving for yet more of a transatlantic look, Sir William Rootes declared the traditional upright radiator parvenu, and Loewy combined with Ryton to conjure up a sort of modernized 1947 Hudson. This became the Mark II Pullman of 1948, styling shared by the new Imperial. The front wings were widely separated from a long, narrow, curved bonnet, the latter swept forward and down to meet a sawn-off grille, all traces of the traditional radiator were eliminated, and flanking grilles with horizontal bars were built into the wing aprons on either side. This facelift would distinguish more and more Humbers. For 1950, the Super Snipe received the treatment, and the 1951 Hawk Mark IV was likewise altered. For the 1953 Super Snipe, the chassis layout and pressed-body style of the concurrent Hawk was adopted. Henceforth both Snipe and Hawk shared these components, though there were significant differences in wheelbase and front/rear sheet metal on some models.

Not rally testing. Fortunately no one took the 'new' Humber Hawk seriously for competition in 1957. Here it's undergoing 'stringent tests at the MIRA testing ground at Nuneaton'. The 4 cylinder Hawk was not sporting

In 1953 a Super Snipe went on a 15 country marathon which it completed in 90 hours. The European countries through which Stirling Moss—asleep?—(and others) passed have their flags attached to the overriders

It was the Mark II Super Snipe, introduced in late 1948, that recaptured a bit of Humber's long-forgotten sporting pretensions, so we should perhaps look at this car in particular.

'There is an appeal about the masterful progress of a big car which handles well,' wrote *The Autocar* in its March 1949 road test. The Super Snipe, the editors continued, was 'a full-size six-seater of impressive and handsome appearance . . . very largely a top gear car, though running on a final-drive ratio of almost exactly 4 to 1, which gives it effortless cruising in the 70mph-plus region . . . Lateral stability for fast cornering is extremely satisfactory and there is a good sense of balance . . . very fine average speed performances can be achieved without the driver feeling that he is making a special effort and without his becoming unusually tired over long distances . . . the steering column gear change is one of the very best of its kind. [Changes are] light and the driver does not find himself in doubt.'

This was strong praise for a car which weighed 3800lb at the kerb and relied on a very understressed engine which produced only 100bhp. Overall, the Humber performed impressively: from rest through the gears to 60 took 22.7 seconds, which was not bad under the circumstances. The Super Snipe had an 80mph capability; driving to its limits was encouraged by upright seats and a properly angled steering wheel. The seats were firm, upholstered in quality, pleated leather. Could this large luxury car succeed in a rally? Two Dutchmen decided to find out.

With encouragement and help from Norman Garrad's competition department, Holland's Maurice Gatsonides and K. S. Barendegt entered a Mark II Super Snipe in the 1950 Monte

The six cylinder Humber Super Snipe engine was tough, smooth and heavy. It did its job well but was essentially no better nor worse than its competitors from BMC, Ford, Vauxhall. Beautifully executed cutaway

Earls Court stand display 1963 for cars built by the Rootes subsidiary, Thrupp & Maberly. Among the exhibits are the Sunbeam Rapier SIV, the new Humber Sceptre, the Hillman Super Minx Convertible, and the Humber Super Snipe SIV

Carlo Rally. (This was the year, the reader may remember, that the Sunbeam-Talbots won a prize for being intact—if not victorious—at the finish, and when Hillman won its class.) A second Humber, entered by Willment-Saville from Glasgow, was also started, but did not finish. Gatsonides/Barendegt started with 90 other cars from Monte Carlo, following a route up to Grenoble, Berne and Strasbourg, across to Amsterdam, and back to the Riviera via Brussels, Paris and Lyons.

Peter Harper (left) and Ian Hall, sizing up their large Humber Super Snipe before the RAC Rally of 1963. They challenged for their class until the gearbox seized at a late stage in the event

The same Super Snipe used by Peter Harper in 1963 tackled the 1964 RAC Rally, driven by Bill Bengry and Barry Hughes, and finished with honour in a class which contained the outright winner

It was typical 'Monte', the weather doing its level worst. Snow began falling south of Paris and was six inches deep at Lyons. Only five cars finished the course without marks: a 1939 Hotchkiss, a trio of Simcas and the Dutchmen's Super Snipe. 'Gatso' had driven a splendid rally, despite the bulk and weight of his car.

This event was covered in Chapter 4, but for Humber's sake might be remembered again. What it came down to was a battle between the Humber, Hotchkiss and Simcas, for only mark-less cars were eligible to compete in the regularity and speed tests at Monte Carlo. Here the Hotchkiss overwhelmed the big Humber, but the latter finished well up on the three Simcas, second overall. It was a moral victory for Rootes. Not only did they win Barclay's Bank Cup for the best British performance—they proved that the Super Snipe would do what *The Autocar* had suggested. Never again did Humber place this high in an international rally, but the point had been proven. While few Super Snipes were entered, those who drove them were never heard to say their cars weren't up to rough and tumble driving.

A new generation of Humbers began in 1957. Again the Loewy people had been busy: the 1957 Hawk was very American in style. The now-monocoque body featured wrap-around windscreen and backlight, hooded headlamps, a large, chromey grille and was very often finished in duotone. (An *Autocar* reader noted that had Humber chamfered the upper corners of the grille they might have retained the former Hawk's distinctive 'face', and protested the hooded headlamps as 'American fripperies'.) The Hawk's original 1944cc engine had been enlarged to 2267cc in 1950 and converted to overhead valves in 1954. In this form it would remain through the Hawk's lifetime, which spanned five series of cars through 1967. Hawks, and the new Snipes that followed, were offered as estate wagons or saloons, the latter with optional division windows, which made them 'touring limousines'.

A more impressive car was the new Super Snipe, which emerged in early 1958, sharing the Hawk's unit body-chassis and 110in wheelbase. Though this was a smaller car dimensionally than its predecessors, there was far more room inside. Unfortunately, the new Snipe was fitted with a gaudy egg-crate grille, by which Rootes hoped to set it apart from the Hawk, and this made it fairly clumsy looking.

One suspects that the design problem stemmed from attempts to copy Detroit. The 1958 Super Snipe, with its duotoned body sides, resembled a 1955 Dodge; the Mark II Snipe of 1960 had moved up to the colour flash styling of the 1957 Dodge. If Rootes were keying their designs to Detroit's, the problem was that the latter were always three years ahead of what they were currently showing.

On the inside, though, the Super Snipe was a gem. Fine burled walnut veneers covered the facia, door fillets and rear-compartment picni tables. Buyers had their choice of West of England cloth or hide upholstery, and the carpeting was best-quality wool.

The Super Snipe (but not the Hawk) was exported to America

Blond hair, big cigar and glasses at the wheel— British disc jockey Jimmy Saville posing in a Humber Imperial of 1965

beginning in 1959, and there it was viewed with quite some enthusiasm by the motoring press. Unlike anything they'd seen from the home country, the Super Snipe was in Yankee parlance 'a compact luxury car'.

Here too, of course, was its marketing difficulty. In America Humber was forced to compete in size and performance with the 'stripped' six-cylinder models of the Big Three—but in price with the higher priced V8 Buicks and Chryslers. It came into the US market at $3995, but quickly rose to $4295 in 1962 and close to $5000 two years later. The only extras offered were a radio (about $100), separate, reclining front seats ($160) and air-conditioning ($295). Initially the Mark II had been available with four-speed manual transmission and with overdrive on the top two gears; but this wasn't chosen by many buyers and with the Series III for 1961, automatic became standard.

'In the light of cold sales figures,' *Road & Track* commented, 'if sheer numerical superiority is the criterion of success, the Humber hasn't made it.' Very few Americans bought Super Snipes. The ones who did were perhaps yearning for the English way of life, for certainly there was here an interior to rival the smoking room at Whites or Boodles. Humber buyers were not concerned with performance—the engine was no larger than the basic Studebaker Lark's, and the performance worse—but what they did appreciate was quality, and this the Super Snipe bespoke in a way American cars hadn't for a generation.

The heart of the Super Snipe—and what set it in a class apart from the Hawk—was its beautifully built, reliable and utterly smooth six-cylinder engine—initially 2651cc, but enlarged to 3 litres through a bore increase on the Series II. Designed for Rootes by Armstrong Siddeley, the big cast-iron unit looked like a 5-litre straight eight under the bonnet. A sophisticated, modern design, it featured hemispherical combustion chambers with opposed valves—inlets on the right, exhausts on the left—operated by pushrods and rockers from a side-mounted camshaft. The Series II, offered for the 1960 model year, switched from Stromberg to Zenith carburation in going up to 3 litres: horsepower was raised from 105 to 121, and torque shot up nearly 20 per cent to 162lb. ft. These changes improved mid-range performance—the Humber was already capable of silent cruising at 80, but it never was a jackrabbit off the line in any of its various manifestations.

The Series II also saw disc front brakes used for the first time—an important improvement. With the 1961–62 Series III there came improved styling: the egg-crate grille was dropped in favour of slim horizontal bars, wrapped completely around the front end. Bizarre duotone schemes ended. The Series IV (1963–64) offered marginally more horsepower and detail refinements. And it was with these big, easy revving 3-litre Humbers that Rootes again sent the marque into competition—in the roughest of all rallies: the East African Safari.

Humber Super Snipe bodyshells arriving at the Thrupp & Maberly works for painting, glazing and trimming, at which this works excelled

The Safari first organized in 1953, is one of the few non-European rallies to have achieved international distinction. High speeds (50mph average) were required on a route that was more rough track than road, passing through the wildest jungle and mountain terrain in Kenya, Uganda and Tanzania. The Safari lasts 90 hours, with only a 6-8 hour break, so drivers are constantly threatened by fatigue.

The organizers specified showroom stock cars, which made the Safari ideal for seeing exactly what the basic production motorcar could take. Initially, classes were based on price, but this mainly encouraged manufacturers to bring in 'Q-ships' at unreasonably low prices. In 1960 the price classifications were eliminated in favour of international displacement classes. This, possibly, is what tempted Rootes to field several teams of Humbers. Hillman Huskys and Sunbeam Rapiers were also entered regularly.

None of the Rootes Group entries ever made Safari results lists during their first two years of activity—1959 and 1960. This has more to do with team planning than the quality of the cars which, as they'd prove in Europe, could take a lot of punishment. Rootes had insisted on using mixed teams of locals and UK drivers, but

Slotting the instrument panel into place in the Humber Imperial's body-shell at the Thrupp & Maberly factory. The 'Selectaride' control above the fitter's head controlled the stiffness settings of the rear suspension dampers

these were never successful. In 1961 four Super Snipes were entered with largely local teams—and it made a difference.

The marathon spanned 3300 miles from Nairobi via a backwoods route to Dar es Salaam and Mombasa, then back to Nairobi for the break. Leg two was to Kampala, Uganda, then back to Nairobi by a different route. Seventy-seven cars started, on what was laughingly called 'The Great North Road'. Immediately some were lost to the errant zebra, hartebeeste or hyena. The first Snipe gave up outside Dar es Salaam with a broken stub axle. Another Snipe was demolished by a 'ngombe' (cow), finishing Humber hopes for a team prize.

Happily, the team of Lee Talbot (a Canadian zoologist doing work in Kenya) and a local named Iqbal managed to avoid the dangers. By the rest stop at Kampala their big Series II was fourth overall, trailing a pair of works Mercedes 220SEs and a brilliant ladies' team of Anne Hall and Lucille Cardwell just 30 seconds ahead in a Ford Zephyr. That was the way they finished, despite an exciting downhill return to Nairobi. The Humber caught the Zephyr on elapsed time in the final minutes, but the ladies had bested Talbot/Iqbal in the special stages, just taking third place. It was a car-breaking ordeal, and out of 38 finishers, Humber was number four.

Lee Talbot lived to fight again in 1962. He was running first in class and seventh overall with a Series III Super Snipe as late as Kampala—the far point on the second leg out of Nairobi. But his unprotected sump was holed, and he retired with his engine seized solid!

Rootes and Humber had lost the discretionary income which permitted such jungle antics by 1964, but there was enough in the pot to permit one more permutation of big Humbers. For the 1965–67 model years, the body was completely redesigned above the waist-line, resulting in the Series IV Hawk, the Series V Super Snipe and a revived Imperial.

Considering that they were dealing with an eight-year-old body, Ryton engineers were quite successful in bringing the Humber up to date. The new roofline was much thinner, rising cleanly from a taller but less 'wrapped' windscreen, raked back towards the boot-lid using a flatter, larger backlight. The side windows were likewise enlarged, while quarter lights at each corner were retained—at the rear they were mounted separately behind the rear doors. The result was an enormous increase in daylight and visibility—and a Humber body that would live for another three years.

Mechanically, engine horsepower and torque were up slightly by the use of a new manifold with twin Zenith-Stromberg carburettors, power steering became standard and a rear anti-roll bar was fitted to the saloon models. As before, estate cars and division limousines had been offered on both Hawk and Snipe lines. Twin carbs gave the Super Snipe a bit more urge. The 0–60 sprint with automatic took about 16 seconds.

No machine could tackle
this job—the hand-crafting
of a vinyl roof covering to a
a big Humber bodyshell

Assembled in London by Thrupp & Maberly, the Imperial was a sort of custom-built ultra-Snipe. Everything Ryton could think of, and find a way to bolt on, was there. Automatic was standard, as were Armstrong Selectaride adjustable rear shock absorbers. Rear passengers faced the usual burled walnut picnic tables, with ashtrays and lighters imbedded in walnut panels on the door arm-rests. Hinged assist straps were mounted over the doors, and universally jointed reading lamps, which switched on when moved from their rest position, provided illumination for the rear passengers. The rear carpet—itself of better quality than most homes—was covered with a deep-pile nylon rug, and there was a separate heating system for the rear seat area. A two-band radio with front and rear speakers, headlamp flashers, fresh-air vents, a dozen-odd courtesy and warning lights, heater–demister, choke and low fuel warning lights were all standard. About the only options a buyer had were seatbelts, whitewall tyres, air-conditioning and either cloth or leather upholstery. (A limousine with division window was also offered, done in leather up front and cloth in the rear.) But sales were not high, and after 1967 these impressive Humbers were gone for good.

Not that Rootes gave up on them willingly. In 1965, just after the new models with their modern superstructures had appeared, the Vehicle Development Department began work on a V8. The Hawk/ Snipe engine bay, of course, offered plenty of room, so a Tiger-type shoehorning was unnecessary.

Because of their growing relationship with Chrysler, Rootes naturally looked towards Highland Park rather than Dearborn for the engine, which was initially slated to be the Plymouth 318 (5.1-litre) V8. This unit had originally appeared on the 1957 Plymouth Fury, in which form it delivered 290bhp. Its immediate predecessor, the 1956 Fury 303 V8, had powered that car to 145mph with special gearing at Daytona Beach, Florida. Off the showroom floor the 1957 318 was capable of 120mph and 0–60 sprints in the eight-second range—in a car fully as heavy, but more streamlined, than the Super Snipe.

In the form tested on the first prototype (labelled SC1 for 'Snipe-Chrysler'), the 318 developed 250bhp at 4400rpm with a single four-choke carburettor; this was bolted to a three-speed manual gearbox connected to a Salisbury rear axle, its ratio higher than the Super Snipe's. Little modification was required for the conversion, aside from relocating engine mounts and grafting Snipe hubs onto the Chrysler halfshafts.

According to Mike Taylor, who reported on a surviving prototype in *Autocar* during 1980, SC1 cruised the MIRA test track at 115mph and had a top speed of 125. This was perhaps more than the Snipe buyer needed, and fuel consumption was dreadful. A Plymouth 273 V8 (4.5 litres) was then tried, using a four-choke carb and developing 196bhp at 5000rpm. This gave a top speed of 118mph. When the four-choke was replaced with a two-choke version, however, bhp dropped to 150 at 4400rpm and top speed to just 104. This was little better than the six-cylinder Snipe's 100mph, though substantially improved acceleration (0–60 in 12 seconds instead of 16). Taylor's research indicates that up to six preproduction 273s were run off.

V8 developments were cut short, however, when Chrysler acquired majority control of Rootes in 1967. The decision was then made not only to abandon the quest for V8 power, but to drop the big Humbers entirely. Despite their recent facelift, the cars were due for a thorough redesign by that time, and management felt the Snipe simply did not warrant the expenditure.

It would seem that a new body should have taken precedence to a V8 engine. The 3-litre six was still very understressed in Series V form, and more performance could have been wrung out of it. On the other hand, the expenses of an engine swap were as nothing compared to the cost of a new body, and it was this—rather than incidental nits like fuel consumption—that condemned the V8 project. Taylor noted that Humber's rival Rover equipped the P5 with an American V8 in late 1967. Though this enhanced the P5's reputation, it did not, in retrospect, do much for sales. Smoothness and refinement were what the Humber or Rover buyer wanted from an engine, and this the sixes already offered.

The marque carried on, however. In 1963 Humber had introduced a smaller model, the Sceptre—essentially a tarted up Hillman Super Minx. In 1967 the Sceptre acquired the Hunter body-

Production of Humber Imperial body/chassis units, in painted and trimmed condition, at the Thrupp & Maberly factory in 1965

No question of moving production lines for the carefully-assembled big Humbers of the 1960s

The last, best, and most fully equipped Humber Imperial of the 1960s. Automatic transmission was standard, the control for which was on the steering column

The sumptuous leather rear seating of the 1965 Humber Imperial, which Rootes aimed squarely at the Jaguar Mk 10 market. Folding picnic tables were attached to the back of the front seats

An artist's rendering of the Humber Imperial, complete with restyled roof and windows, the last derivative of a car announced in 1959

shell, and remained in production as such until 1976. But Sceptres were not really Humbers in the traditional sense. It was a sad way to say goodbye to a marque which, if not one of the great ones, had always stood for quality and value.

Contemporary collector tastes render the Vanden Plas 3-litre and Rover P5 far more sought-after than the Humber Super Snipe and Imperial. This seems to involve body styling. Collector market prices for Vanden Plas models are gamey and high pitched; Rover P5s are in the same league. A Humber Super Snipe and even an Imperial cost half as much in comparable condition. It is significant that both Vanden Plas and Rover stuck to traditional styling approaches, with big, four-square radiator grilles. Rootes 'went Detroit' with its Humbers. Had the Super Snipe early on acquired a traditional front end, it would be far more sought after today.

On the plus side, the Super Snipe and Imperial are two of the more affordable luxury cars on the collector market, offering refinement and luxury that is difficult, if not impossible, to duplicate for the price.

6

Alpine: Arrival of the forward look

Virgil Exner was the only car stylist whose name became a house-hold word in America. Exner was known, to his disadvantage in later days, as 'father of the tailfin', which he instituted as Chrysler's chief of design in 1956. Exner's theories were more involved than the simple uplift of a heretofore turned-down posterior: he thought fins abetted stability at speed (they did, but only upwards of 80mph or so) and were the obvious way to design motorcars in the jet age. Whatever its physical properties, the tailfin gave 'definition' to the previously undistinguished rears of what Ken Purdy called that 'turgid river of jelly-bodied clunkers'—with which we Yanks plied the highways in the fifties. Tailfins were very 'in', make no mistake. What Exner called the 'Forward Look' did wonders for Chrysler sales in 1957, bringing the company a market slice it hadn't enjoyed since the forties.

Given Lord Rootes' obsession with the American way of motor-ing, one supposes it was natural that he would take the tailfin to his heart at the time it held sway. After all, even mighty General Motors was striving (and eventually succeeding) to out-fin Chrysler. The Loewy people, of course, had introduced the tailfin to Rootes products with the Series II Rapier, inspired by Stude-baker, which in turn had been inspired by Virgil Exner's Chrysler products. So Rootes were psychologically ready for a generically finned job by the time a new Sunbeam Alpine was being designed.

The Loewy Studios had by now completed their contract, but they did have some indirect influence on the new Alpine. Its styling fell to Swindon-born Kenneth Howes, whose first design experi-ence had occurred under Clare Hodgman at the Loewy London office shortly after the war. From there, Howes had spent time in the States, both at Loewy's Studebaker studio in South Bend and at Ford Styling in Dearborn. In 1956 he had returned to England and Rootes, where he worked under the direction of ornamentation specialist Jeff Crompton, who in turn reported to Ted White. Howes was assisted in the Alpine programme by Roy Axe, who in the late seventies would come to head Chrysler Styling in Detroit. We can see that the design of the car was eminently transatlantic.

One of the very first Sunbeam Alpines of 1959—one of the original 'XVC' cars—these cars being assembled by Armstrong-Siddeley at their Parkside factory

By contrast, this is a later 1964 Series IV Alpine, at the time when the car was at its best, pre-Chrysler influence of any sort. It's in left-hand drive form and photographed in America. The series lasted well

Howes and Axe conceived a dart-shaped car that was essentially 'pure', which was a rather direct contrast to the Loewy-inspired Minx/Gazelle/Rapier line, which were more 'decorated'. Tailfins were almost *de rigueur* from the first; given their dominance across the pond, they were met with the enthusiastic approval of Lord Rootes.

The new Alpine progressed from quarter-scale clay model to finished, full-size wooden mock-up with very minor changes during 1957. Painted bright red, the mock-up was duly placed, Loewy-style, on a turntable at the Rootes studios. Lord William and Sir Reginald approved the car for production in December 1957. Manifestly it was the work of Ken Howes. Mike Taylor, in his book on the Sunbeam Tiger, quotes White as giving Howes 80 per cent of the credit, Axe the balance.

'I think Ken did a remarkable job on the Alpine,' said his former South Bend boss, Bob Bourke. 'I remember him as a likeable young man, great fun off duty, but very serious about his design work, which he was just learning then, of course. His ideas about cars were not flamboyant in the American sense, rather they were refined. I always admired his Alpines, and the other models that developed from them.'

The design was certainly slippery enough, testing favourably at the MIRA wind tunnel, with a coefficient of drag well below those of the rival MGA and TR3. Due to heavy developmental commitments at Coventry, Rootes farmed out the make-ready engineering to Armstrong Siddeley, a neighbour with whom they had good working relationships. Siddeley had just completed the new

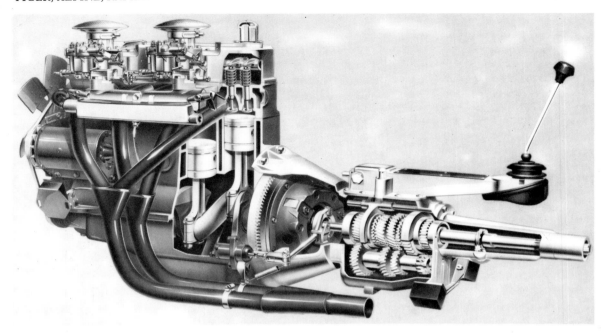

Humber 3-litre six, with its sophisticated inclined overhead valves, hemispherical combustion chambers and special push-rod valve gear. Johnny Johnson, the initial Rootes project engineer attached to the Alpine, was shortly superseded by Alec Caine, who would direct all Alpine development through the final Mark V.

The test period revealed few problems. Chiefly, these were body vibration forward of the scuttle and carburettor leaks where the inlet manifold joined the alloy cylinder head. The latter were quickly attended to by Zenith's man, Charles Fisher. To stop the vibrating, Rootes engineering director Peter Ware decreed diagonal strengthening members mounted between the bulkhead and the inner wings. Historical articles on the Tiger have sometimes intimated that the Alpine was nevertheless a flimsy package; while much strengthening went on to meet the added performance stress in the Tiger, nothing could be further from the truth. In fact, the Alpine was a very rigid car for its class, and Rootes salesmen joyously took customers for rides over railroad crossings to prove it.

No matter how you feel about tailfins, you will probably grant that the new Alpine was a nice-looking car. Given the weight of professional opinion among designers interviewed for this book, Howes did an excellent piece of work—modest fins combined with ultra-clean, curved sides and a beautiful little half-oval grille with neat horizontal bars. The bonnet rose rapidly to meet the scuttle, giving the driver a very near view of what was about to pass underneath. Ken Howes's blank-slate design ticket meant that he was relatively free to sketch in provision for roll-up side windows, something the Germans and Italians had no problems with on

The Mark I Alpine engine and gearbox. Twin down-draught Zenith carburettors and tubular exhaust are different from the contemporary Rapier's, as is the cylinder head. No overdrive is shown here

The first series Alpine with wire wheels and factory hardtop. Whitewall tyres continue the company's American obsession

sports cars, but which the British seemed notably recalcitrant to render. By 1960 the dubious traditions of snap-on side curtains had lost whatever appeal they once had, particularly in the all-important North American market. Since the new Alpine was a fresh concept, there seemed no reason to slight it with this throwback to the past, nor to trouble it with a complicated, ill-fitting soft top, either.

Concerning the latter, Rootes production engineers were ingenious. Whereas BMC and Standard-Triumph sports cars' tops were of the separate-bows-and-take-off variety, the Alpine's was permanently attached to the car. To lower it, you simply unhooked a pair of over-centre windscreen header catches and slipped out a set of cantrails which served to stiffen the outer edges. Then, you hinged-open three metal panels: a big one at the rear and two small flanking ones—exposing a little 'nest' into which the entire top/framework folded. One had to be a bit careful so as not to crease or scratch the Plexiglas rear window, but in all it was a simple operation, and in a quick rainstorm one needn't even bother with the cantrails. Saleswise, this was a tremendous advantage.

This writer bought a Mark II Sunbeam Alpine off the floor from a Studebaker dealer on Staten Island, New York, in late 1962, and drove it some 40,000 miles over the next two years. The people who sold Rootes products in America at that time tended to be Studebaker or AMC dealers—or worse, BMC or Triumph dealers. The domestic Big Three had all the business they could handle selling American cars, and Chevrolet agencies naturally wanted to restrict two-seater sales to Corvettes. This proved troublesome to

Mark II Alpine of 1961 in North American trim. Distinguished appearance, with swoopy tail fins and smooth lines, sold the car to many Americans. Triple eared knock-off hubs helped too

This team of privately entered Sunbeam Alpines tackled the Monte Carlo Rally of 1960, but without success

customers, because the rank-and-file Studebaker dealer in 1962 was pretty much nearing rigor mortis; in taking on a Rootes franchise, he was only trying to ward off the inevitable, which translated into indifferent service and sporadic spares supplies, as I quickly learned.

Compared to the Triumph TR I'd just traded in, the Alpine was a revelation—of how pleasant a sports car could be with a few minor concessions. It's difficult, of course, to compare a classically sprung, wind-in-the-face TR with the softer, civilized Alpine, but certain characteristics are worth contrasting. I found right away that no normal Alpine would go quite as fast as a TR3—in a straight line. But its roadholding was clearly superior, especially over the wash-board surfaces New York City was—is—blessed with. This a TR3, perhaps untidily driven by a friend, learned with consternation one bright spring day on Staten Island.

As to liveability, the Alpine had it all over the TR. In a rainstorm it was heaven to reach back, flick open the metal panels and snap the top in place; in spring and autumn, I learned, it was actually possible to adjust cockpit temperature without fiddling with a tap attached to the engine block. I found it was possible to have a sports car *and* comfortable seats, roll-up windows, a pleasant ride and all the other things sports cars were supposed to lack. I said as much to one Fred K. Gamble of Standard-Triumph's owners' club—much to his amusement and much to the improvement of my own enthusiasms.

Being what it was, of course, made life with the Alpine a constant face-off between the owner and Joseph Lucas. There was the battery that went belly-up within a year, the headlamps that kept burning out, the heater blower that didn't, the wiper motor I had to leave unparked to be sure of a restart in the wet, or hit with a hammer to get it going again. Still the Alpine, then priced in the US at about £900, was tremendous value for money. I bettered my motoring only when I traded up to a Tiger.

The truth of the matter is that few circuit-raced the Alpine in the UK. In North America there were necessarily many more. Here's a typical race prepared example, that of Don Sesslar (it's 'semi-official factory supported) the F-Production champion in 1964

Let us have a look, now, at what Rootes wrought, commencing with the structure of the beast, quoting the rationale of Rootes-USA in early advertising:

'For a car to be strong, the chassis and body had [previously] to be heavy. Not only did this make for greater sprung weight, but under driving stresses the chassis developed its own momentum and vector, and the body *its* own. The separate masses would then fight each other, with resultant difficult handling, a relatively weak structure and short body/chassis life. The solution came with pioneering research [they could thank the Rapier for this] into integral construction. Using newly developed light metals, Sunbeam designers combined the body and chassis into a single unit, attached suspension fore and aft and virtually eliminated the chassis. [This] very neatly solves the historic difficulty encountered in designing open sports cars. In losing the stress-absorbing function of the roof and side pillars, torsional strength was consequently decreased, rigidity diminished, stresses were unequally transmitted into the main frame and the entire unit progressively weakened. But integral construction permits designers to keep the roof, retain the stress-absorbing function of the side pillars, and use them in the main frame. Keep the roof in an open car? Yes, in the floor!'

Illustrating a Sunbeam shell (which used a Hillman Husky undertray and wheel wells), this advert pointed out that the floor was recessed below the body sills, forming a box-like structure of considerable strength and rigidity, what they called 'an inverted roof'. Aside from this there were the benefits of a lower centre of gravity, and more legroom—and the disadvantage, as in most unit body cars, of a tendency to rust. Yes, Alpines (and Tigers) rusted, and for enthusiasts in the market today, this is the most crucial consideration. But unit construction unquestionably made the Alpine tighter and quieter than the rank-and-file middling-priced sports cars of the day, including both MG and Triumph.

95

Harrington's first publicity shot, for themselves, appeared in 1961. Standard disc wheels and hub caps aren't as attractive as wire wheels. The Harrington conversion inspired many other manufacturers to offer coupé-like hardtops, even fixed heads

Peter Harper overseeing preparation on his 1961 Harrington Alpine before the Le Mans Sports car race. Jack Walton and Ernie Beck are working on the car. That is one of the team's Series III Rapier rally cars in the background

Into this new unit body went componentry straight off the Ryton spares shelves. The Series I's 1494cc engine was, of course, Rapier-bred, but there was a difference: a cast aluminium alloy head of new design, with a rather novel valve order. The two centre intakes were side by side, with the other intake and exhaust opening altering away from centre,* and the valves were inclined at a 4.5-degree angle to the vertical. This was done, Rootes stated, to provide a better port shape, improve gas flow and avoid hot spots. The exhaust system was a twin-branch affair, with ducting from cylinders 1/4 and 2/3 melding into a single tailpipe. Carburation was via twin 36 WIP2 Zenith downdraughts, with water jackets incorporated at their bases to provide controlled induction heating, Unlike the Rapier, the carbs used individual wire gauze air cleaners.

* Valve positions: e-i-e-i-i-e-i-e; normally they were: e-i-i-e-e-i-i-e.

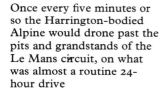

Once every five minutes or so the Harrington-bodied Alpine would drone past the pits and grandstands of the Le Mans circuit, on what was almost a routine 24-hour drive

3000RW was one of the original 1961 Le Mans Series II Alpines (3001RW was the other). It had the Harrington hardtop style, finished sixteenth overall, and won the Index of Thermal Efficiency prize that year, driven by Peter Harper and Peter Procter

The cylinder block was stiffened with three extra ribs between sump flange and crankshaft, and the crank was made of high-tensile steel. Connecting rod bearings were of lead-indium alloy. To help keep things cool under the bonnet and behind the minimal grille, a six-bladed fan and cross-flow radiator were adopted; the header tank was made separate and moved back to permit the plunging bonnet. The gearbox, Hillman Husky-derived, was a remote control four-speed with close-ratio gearing and modified gear tooth spiral angles. Laycock overdrive was available, operating on third and top, providing a moderate 25 per cent step-up, this giving the car six effective forward speeds.

The Alpine was the first Rootes product to be equipped with front disc brakes, though they soon became commonplace; the handbrake, as expected, was located on the driver's offside. Front suspension, Rapier-like, was entirely conventional: ifs via coils and unequal-length wishbones with rollbar and telescopic dampers; rigid rear axle with lever-type shock absorbers and semi-elliptic leaf springs.

A great deal of ergonomic thought went into the Alpine 'office', as this writer smugly pointed out in 1962 to the Triumph people. The door panels were plain, but had strong pull-grips, and one could order armrests (which were more useful as strengthening members than elbow-platforms). The rest of the upholstery was very de luxe: deep, pleated PVC bucket seats, luxurious, thick carpeting, and a facia trimmed top and bottom with padded vinyl. The facia itself was a silvery grey affair which housed the obligatory speedo/rev counter under the steering wheel, a smaller oil pressure gauge helpfully centred between them. Inboard were a water temperature and fuel gauge; a large central plug could be removed

97

to install an optional clock, and another bung-hole at the driver's offside could take an ammeter—always very useful when one is dealing with Mr Lucas.

There weren't many major options to the Alpine, which cost £972 with tax when first released in Britain. One could order centre-lock wire wheels for £38, electric overdrive for £60, a tonneau cover (*sans* steering wheel recess, which looked clumsy when snapped on) for £10 and a neat hardtop with broadly wrapped Plexiglas rear backlight. The latter cost just £60 and was nicely finished with a vinyl headliner. There was a heater/demister controlled by sliding levers which poked through the dash, and lots of room was contained between facia and gearbox tunnel for radio equipment. Buyers could get an upholstered 'rear seat', but even

In 1961, Rootes entered two Alpines for the Le Mans 24 Hour race. This was the conventionally-shaped car, fitted with the detachable hardtop, and driven by Paddy Hopkirk and Peter Jopp

Although the Harrington Le Mans floor pan, nose, screen and doors were standard Alpine, the rest was new, and coachbuilt at the Harrington factory on the south coast of England

Rootes admitted this was strictly kid-stuff. One untoward note: the passenger glovebox had no lid; but part of it was cut away to provide the passenger with a handy grab bar.

One of those who early enthused over a Series I Alpine was the inimitable Tom McCahill, longtime auto editor of *Mechanix Illustrated* and virtual inventor of the 0–60 sprint on his side of the pond. A McCahill test was always different from everybody else's, eminently quotable.

'Uncle Tom' was a big, bold man, and he had two complaints about the Alpine: there should have been an adjustable steering wheel (especially for chaps with biggish bellies), and the throttle pedal was too high on the left-hand drive model he tried. Beyond this, he couldn't have liked it more. 'I found this car grooving through the corners with all the ease of a tomahawk going through a soft scalp.' [You were warned he was different.] 'On a well-known turnpike in the wee hours this little red Glockenspiel clocked 102.4mph over a measured mile with a slight quartering side wind. . . . At high speeds this car gets down the pike like a paper clip from a two-pound test rubber band . . . 0–60mph needs 13.2 seconds [McCahill's time was among the more rapid]. This won't cause you much embarrassment unless you bump into a nasty guy in a Pontiac.

'In summing up, the Sunbeam Alpine is one of those cars that comes along very seldom . . . its personality is brimming over with swashbuckle and it has more character than an old movie with an entire cast of Lionel Barrymores. [It's not] the greatest sports car I've ever twirled down the pike, but at $2599 it's the best offering dollar-for-dollar since the first Austin-Healey hit here in the early '50s. As a top rally car and possibly production class [SCCA] sports car, it's going to take a lot to beat it.'

What Tom McCahill liked in 1959 was only better in mid-1960, when the Series II Alpine replaced the original. On the surface, the two cars looked the same. The most obvious identifying characteristic was the window channel for the door glass: stubby on the Series I, full-length on the Series II. But inside and under the skin, the Alpine had improved in several ways.

Overshadowing—in this writer's opinion—the Series II's useful increase in power was Rootes deft handling of owner and road test feedback. For once in the history of the industry, what drivers thought had really mattered. *Road & Track*, for example, had complained about a bolt-upright driving position on the first Alpine, saying that one's legs had to fit around, rather than under, the steering wheel. *Voilà*; Rootes raised the wheel and tilted the seatbacks at a more comfortable angle. The long window channels were also a result of customer comment about Series I window rattles. With the glass rolled down, though, these thin, bright-metal spikes threatened to give the unwary a nasty poke in the eye. The sum total was, however, an improved, even more comfortable Sunbeam Alpine.

Just a detail—the 'Le Mans' badges, and the 'Harrington-England' decals identify a true Harrington-modified Sunbeam Alpine

Mechanically, Rootes provided added urge by boring out the engine to 1592cc (81.5 × 76.2mm), producing two more horse-power (now 85.5) and five more pounds-feet of torque (now 94). 'Officially, the changes here have been very minor,' said *Road & Track*. '. . . indeed, the engine feels de-tuned—an impression which is confirmed by the fact that maximum power comes in 300rpm below the old 83.5bhp peak of 5300rpm . . . but we would judge that the engine pulls very near its peak over a wide rpm range . . . the new model is also much improved in smoothness, and, most important, the engine will 'blip' up to speed very quickly, whereas it was definitely sluggish in this respect before.'

Today's Motor Sports, another American magazine, said the added torque provided 'a real shot in the arm. Where a Mark I with 1500cc would just break 15 seconds in the traditional 0–60 test; the Mark II will do it in under 12 seconds.' This was probably an exaggeration—most tests gave 0–60 times of around 14.5 and 13.5 seconds respectively—but does indicate the improvements made.

In America, the Alpine made its debut in SCCA production sports car Class G-Production in 1960. Baltimore's Vince Tamburo, with minimal help from the factory, was national class champion that year, starting off on the right foot. On paper the Series II Alpine should have been better than the first model, and it was—but so was the competition. On the strength of Tamburo's performance, and with the Series II's displacement increase, SCCA bumped the Alpine up to Class F–Production in 1961. Here, competitors like the Deutsch-Bonnet and Alfa Romeo Giulietta barred the Alpine from top money until 1964, when Ohioan Don Sesslar won the national championship. In 1965, when SCCA broke down the titles by divisions, another Ohioan, Dan Carmichael, won for Sunbeam in the Central Division, tying with a Volvo P-1800. The Series V's 1725cc moved the Alpine up to Class E after 1965, however, which ended the car's success in national racing.

Regretfully, the Alpine's rally career in Europe may be dealt with in almost as few words as its trackcraft in America. Things started off well enough: an Alpine won its class (Grand Touring, 1300–1600cc) in the 1960 Monte Carlo Rally and was third in class at both the Tour of Ireland and Alpine Rally. In 1961 the Monte Carlo class win was repeated, and another Alpine won the Scottish Rally outright. After that, the record quickly dried up, and burrowers into dusty magazines find that Rootes began to rely heavily again on the now-fast-being-outdated Rapier. While

Noted German-based American journalist Jerry Sloniger, wringing out the first Harrington Le Mans on the Goodwood racing circuit. In this shot, the car is rolling considerably

works-backed Alpines did race, and often won, in production class events at tracks like Brands Hatch and Silverstone, after 1961 they were mostly absent from the rally circuit.

The reason for this has less to do with the Alpine's viability as a rally car than with the corporate sales situation. Management, stated Lewis Garrad, 'were determined that the volume of the Rapier would be such that we needed that sort of push behind it. They thought the Alpine would sell on its appearance—and as a matter of fact it did. It was an attractive-looking car, and was thought of as a tarty car, which the young man was bought by his Daddy. But the Rapier needed a constant promotion. That was the main reason for concentrating on rallying the Rapier. It was more of a workhorse.'

This sort of policy might have been fine for European and Commonwealth markets, but by the time the Alpine arrived, Rapier sales in America were insignificant. Some Rootes dealers didn't even stock them; under persistent demands by a money-waving customer, they just might be persuaded to order one. The Alpine was the sporty car to sell to Americans, and in the US sports car market, competition success *did* matter. There was a way, though, to attack this: run Alpines at the long-distance marathons, Sebring and Le Mans.

Tucked away into one corner of the Earls Court Motor Show of 1962 was the Harrington display of five differently-equipped Harrington Alpines. The car in the foreground, of course, is a Harrington Le Mans

Gregor Grant (editor of *Autosport*) and Peter Pilsworth in their Alan Fraser entered Alpine at the start of the 1962 RAC Rally. Car is shod with the then obligatory Dunlop SP3 radial tyres. Their grip was excellent but their life was short

For the Twelve Hours of Sebring in March 1961, three Alpines were entered. The drivers were Procter/Harper, Theodoll/Barrette and Hopkirk/Jopp. All three finished the gruelling Florida enduro, with Procter well up among the leaders at seventeenth overall, completing 171 laps at a 74.9mph average. Rootes-USA crowed loudly in full-page ads: 'While cars costing up to $20,000 dropped out with mashed gearboxes, or lost ground by having to change as many as 20 tyres . . . a Sunbeam Alpine proved its stamina and reliability with an outstanding performance . . . That makes the budget priced Alpine the equivalent of middleweight champion. It beat every car in its price class.'

A piece of deft advertising, this. The Alpine *did* beat every car selling for $2595, all right. But it had been bested by an Austin-Healey Sprite ($1795) and two MGAs ($2440). Yet Sebring was a decent performance, in that every other car ahead of Procter's was far more exotic and expensive.

But Sebring was mere preparation for the big one in France the following June. Alick Dick's Standard-Triumph had for several years been proving the merits of winning one's class at Le Mans. Dick once told the writer that the sole purpose of Triumph's efforts there was publicity: 'It meant a great deal to the buyer to know he was driving in something related, possibly remotely, to a 24 Hours

Privately entered this time, Gregor Grant accompanied by London car dealer Cliff Davis half way through the 1962 Monte Carlo Rally. Note the re-located petrol filler cap on the rear wing

champion.' Possibly with the Triumph experience in mind, Rootes set about preparing Alpines for Sarthe.

Lewis Garrad has pointed out that his father—and Rootes—had never entertained the idea of a Le Mans entry before 1961: 'In fact I don't think he'd ever been to Le Mans. It started when a distributor in Paris wrote Dad with the suggestion. We had the Alpine by that time, so this was kicked around.

'We took a basic Alpine to the MIRA track at Lindley, and ran it for 24 hours, using Peters Harper, and Procter plus Jimmy Ashworth and myself as drivers. We drove it round and round for 24 hours and it didn't break. Then Father went to see Brian Rootes, who was director of export sales, and got the go-ahead. We decided to take two cars, one standard and one modified.' The latter stemmed from an intriguing side-project already under way: the Alpine GT.

The coachbuilding firm of Thomas Harrington Ltd., on Old Shoreham Road, Hove, Sussex, dated back to 1897, when it began supplying custom bodies to the carriage trade. Although Lewis Garrad recalled that Harringtons 'were used to playing around with aluminium', what really interested them in 1961 was fibreglass—and the chances of using it to create a semi-coachbuilt GT model of the Alpine. Such a car, managing director Clifford Harrington informed Rootes' Alec Caine, would have inviting sales prospects. (It would also provide helpful employment for Harrington Ltd.)

Caine was impressed with the idea and so, in due course, was Lord Rootes. In early 1961, Harringtons were purchased by the Robins and Day Group, wholly owned by the Rootes family, who placed George Hartwell in charge. Hartwell, the wizard who had turned stodgy Rapiers into rally giants, interested himself in tuning modifications, while Harrington stylist Ron Humphries set about designing the new GT.

The initial (1961) model, sold exclusively through Harrington and not exported, was an Alpine *sans* bootlid and roof mechanism, fitted with a fibreglass fastback. Progenitor of numerous bolt-on fastbacks for popular sports cars, it was interesting though hardly beautiful. The fastback extended rearwards from the windscreen header over most of the luggage compartment; a hinged lid finished off the conversion. The strong 'break' between roofline and bootlid and the high roof combined with the unaltered Alpine tailfins, added up to a fairly bizarre impression.

After one got over the styling—if one could—the rest of the spec attracted. The interior was fitted with Microcell bucket seats; the driver faced a Carlotti wood-rimmed steering wheel (which necessitated a separate horn lever on the column) and a Crypton electronic rev counter. The little coupé was finely finished, and priced competitively: £1225, £1300 and £1440 for three stages of tune. Harrington announced a production goal of 'not more than 250 per year', and meant it: in the abbreviated 1961 period, about 150 Alpine GTs were built.

The Stage 1 kit for the Alpine had already been developed by Hartwell. It consisted of a high-lift camshaft, stronger valve springs, reshaped and polished valve throats and induction ports, cleaned-up exhaust ports and a manifold matched to the cylinder head. This unit delivered 88bhp at 5500rpm.

Stage 2, also a Rootes kit, comprised Stage 1 plus a lightened flywheel and heavy-duty, nine-spring clutch, these balanced as a unit with the crankshaft; horsepower was 93 at 5700rpm.

Stage 3 was Hartwell's work for the Harrington—and for the coupé used at Le Mans. This engine had, in addition to Stages 1 and 2, a high-compression cylinder head (9.5:1 at first, later 10.2:1) plus two double-choke 40mm Weber carburettors, resulting in 100bhp at 6200rpm—the fastest-ever works Alpine. *Autosport*, which tested a Stage 3 Harrington in April 1961, achieved 110mph and a 17.9-second quarter-mile, real 2-litre performance from 1.6.

All three tuning stages met FIA regulations; it was possible to go even further, though they didn't at the time. Mating the 'Hartwell head' with the Rootes special flat-top pistons jumped the CR to 12:1, and with the recommended Iskenderian cam, horsepower was in the range of 120. Regretfully, none of these 'Stage 4' engines were homologated, nor do they appear to have been tested.

After Norman Garrad received a Le Mans go-ahead from Brian Rootes, he asked Harrington to develop a racing coupé based on their Alpine GT. The Hove people duly fitted a GT with sunken headlamps covered by flush-fitting Plexiglas shields and a full undertray to improve streamlining. This was turned over to Garrad, who hurriedly began race-testing with the 24 Hours less than 90 days away.

Initial tests of stock Alpine GTs in Stage 2 form had shown 0–60 times around 12.5 seconds, though of course the Stage 3 GT was quicker. Its most astonishing improvement was in top-end acceleration: the 70–90mph leap could be done 11 seconds quicker than the Mark II Alpine with Stage 2, and some 15 seconds quicker with Stage 3. In April, the Garrad team took their cars to the Sarthe circuit itself for a pre-race trial, but they were disappointed: 'The cars weren't anywhere quick enough for a class win,' Lewis Garrad said, 'which wasn't really so surprising after all.'

'We came back and said okay, we're not going to win, that's for sure. But if we do our job properly we can make some petrol economy! We had another long talk with Engineering, and thought we could compete for the Index of Thermal Efficiency.'

'Bear in mind,' Garrad said, 'that not one of us had been to Le Mans apart from the April test weekend. We couldn't buy expertise, we hadn't the money. We knew nothing about the intricacies of the organizers, who were the living end. For instance, we knew nothing about the rule that the boot has to have a wooden suitcase fitted in it.' Thus these babes entered the Le Mans woods.

'We took two cars and about 30 people to Le Mans,' Garrad continued. 'We'd borrowed a lovely blue caravan with red velour carpets and curtains. I towed it from Coventry to Le Mans behind a Super Snipe estate car, and we arrived for scrutineering. It was unbelievable.

'The Ferrari people were there at the same time, and they too were having trouble with the suitcase rule. They claimed their cars had adequate luggage space to meet the standards. In my very limited French I heard the Ferrari men say to the organizers,

On occasion, top racing drivers like Stirling Moss (shirtless, second from the left) were attracted to racing Alpines in North American events. The other 'person-ality' in the picture is Jack Brabham, at the tail, head down, in sun glasses

American F-Production racing was tough for the Alpine. The MGA and the Porsche 356 (ignore the DB Panhard behind the Alpine) were the opposition. Driver Bill Kneeland was known for his wild antics in Alpine no. 81

"Look, that's sufficient as far as we're concerned, and you either accept it or we go back to Modena." They did! I thought blimey, if they can do it so can I! So I said, "Either you accept [our luggage provision] or we're off to Coventry." The Ferrari guy, a very friendly bloke, agreed with me, and we said, "Look ------ the suitcase." So we got over that problem.

'We had also put a huge great inlet on the petrol filler, and that, too, wasn't in the regulations. We didn't even have the correct fire extinguisher. We learned damn quickly, though. We took over a garage and did terrific work in three days by very basic methods. We found that the organizers would change their minds every five minutes. It wasn't until the Ferrari episode that I realized how we had to approach them. We got through it finally, and in practice the cars were quite quick. But the thing that was attractive was their economy.'

Whilst to some it may seem incongruous that Rootes could have placed their hopes on mere fuel economy at Le Mans, the fact is that a good showing of any kind there meant tremendous publicity. Le Mans is the ultimate endurance test. Cars that survive its unrelenting pounding are big box office. If the Sunbeams could win the Efficiency Index they would have to finish; to finish *and* win would quite satisfy the sales folk back home. It was a crucial test, but a very new kind of challenge to the Garrad team.

While Peter Harper circulated consistently in the Seacrest green GT, Hopkirk's conventional Alpine was soon in with a failed main bearing. Again the formidable Le Mans organizers faced the team.

The 1962 Le Mans Alpines were still basically Series II models, but had a different squared-off style of tail. This was the Paddy Hopkirk-Peter Jopp car (Hopkirk driving in this shot), which lapped at 98.6mph in the early stages. Teammates Harper and Procter finished fifteenth in the sister car

'Judith Jackson, who by this time was Peter Jopp's girlfriend, was our interpreter,' Garrad recalled. 'In her best French, she asked the authorities if we could change the oil, since we had to take the sump off and put a new main bearing in. No, they said, we hadn't done enough laps! You can imagine trying to tell the French organizers that they were expecting us to take the sump off, put in a new main bearing, and use the same oil. It's a bit dotty. Judith and they had a right old harangue, with lots of arm-waving and all the rest.'

The organizers were adamant—no new oil! What to do? 'We used the old oil, of course,' Garrad said ruefully. 'We had to filter it, so we used one of Judith's stockings!' Norman Garrad's insistence on having female expertise had paid off again.

Meanwhile, the Harrington kept going round 'like a clockwork mouse. Peter was used to rallying, so he wasn't out to break all the records; rather, he was doing what he did best, putting in very routine, very regular laps. If you told him to drive down the M1 at 30mph he'd do it. He had an enormous standing with the crowd.

'The car was using very little petrol and causing no trouble. We'd practised the pit stops, and had them down pat. It was purely: change the oil, put the fuel in, and off you go. I remember about nine in the morning, with 21 hours completed, the chief organizer told me if we souped our car up a little we'd beat Porsche for the fuel economy thing. Great delight! We ran up a sign that said 'plus 500 revs to beat X' and sure enough, up came 500rpm. Peter of course, was very disciplined. The car just kept going round and round. Frankly, we couldn't believe it! It gave us no trouble at all.

'They had a computer printing results, and for reasons known only to the French, at noon Sunday it stopped printing. We didn't know where the hell we were—hadn't a clue. And the race was finished.

'I walked into the organizers' office. There was Bob Hanzler of the Porsche team, rattling away in French and talking to me in English: "You haven't gone quick enough," he said. "We have beaten you." I was disappointed, but retorted, "Who says?" He replied, "I says." I told him, "Well, you're not the organizer!"

'Anyway, a fellow came out and produced the result. Sure enough, we had won the Index of Thermal Efficiency. I walked slowly back to the pits, found Dad and the team sitting there stunned. They couldn't believe it. We'd won!

'Raymond Baxter of the press joined us, and I reckon we got drunk that night. It was unbelievable. We didn't realize the car had guts at all.'

The results added up to one of Rootes all-time great competition performances—vindicating once and for all any charges that the great Sunbeam-Talbot heritage was dead. When Harper charged across the finish line, he and Procter had averaged 91mph for 2181.9 miles, with only *nine minutes* for pit stops. They hadn't even changed a tyre. It was, perhaps, Sunbeam's greatest race day since long before the war.

Riding the crest of post-race enthusiasm, Harrington commissioned Ron Humphries to design an even more complete GT for 1962, the 'Type B'. This was introduced at Earls Court in October as the Sunbeam Harrington Le Mans. ('Harrington' was dropped, along with the exterior 'steering wheel' badges on at least some models.) It proved that given enough time and a decent budget, Humphries could create a stunning shape unlike anything else on the road.

In contrast to the Alpine GT or 'Type A', the new coupé was based on an Alpine with its entire body-top aft of the doors sawn off. A new, elegant fibreglass fastback was bolted in place, covering the car from windscreen header to rear bumper, eliminating not

Tommy Wisdom at the wheel of the ex-Le Mans 'duck-tail' Alpine, in the early stages of the 1963 Monte Carlo Rally, where the team were defeated by incredibly wintry conditions

Sunbeam Venezia Coupé—a combination of normal (Rapier-length) wheelbase, floor pan and power train, and Superleggera Touring coachwork, first sold in 1963

only the vestigial bootlid but the tailfins as well. To hide the seam where plastic top met metal body, Humphries brilliantly laid down a thin piece of brightwork, extending it through the doors and front wings, where it ended in an arrow motif. Behind the pivoting rear lights he placed small extractor vents, trimmed with bright metal on some models, and on others bare.

The Harrington Le Mans offered dramatic upgrading in the Alpine office, with Microcell buckets and special door panels containing substantial arm/leg rests and map pockets. The Carlotti wood-rimmed wheel was matched by a walnut dash, including a hinged, lockable lid for the Alpine's yawning glovebox. 'The whole assembly is weather-tight and rattle free,' said *Sports Car Graphic*, 'despite the mixing of plastic and metal in manufacture.'

The Le Mans sold in the US for $4000 and in England for £1495 including tax. Wire wheels (£40) and Dunlop RS5 tyres (£9) were options. Overdrive, initially listed as an option, was soon made standard, adding £62 to the price. Fitted with the Stage 2 engine, the car had a top speed of around 105. Its sole tractability problem was a certain reluctance to get under way at low rpm, due to the lightened flywheel. Cruising at 80mph it was a delight. Hove had created the definitive mid-displacement Grand Touring car.

Two Harringtons were entered for Le Mans 1962, but Rootes failed to repeat their Index win. 'We made a complete mess of it,' said Lewis Garrad. 'We thought in 1962 that we knew it all—but money was running out and we didn't have enough, really. We used pretty stock cars and didn't do it properly.' Yet Harper and Procter covered 50 miles more than in 1961, finishing fifteenth overall and seventh in class. And all but one of the higher finishers (a Morgan) were far more expensive than the Harrington. Garrad nevertheless reflected: 'It taught me a lesson. If you are going to do something, do it well, because you can't go back to it after.'

From the rear, the Venezia coupé had a definite family resemblance to the Series IV Sunbeam Alpine sports car, announced in 1964

True to their intent, Harrington built around 250 Type B models, while Ron Humphries worked on a future development. The high cost of manufacturing the Le Mans caused him to cut corners with his 'Type C', a cross between the fastback Le Mans and the notchback Alpine GT. An opening backlight was retained, but so were those fins; the bootlid did not open, but tapered to a shape similar to the Type B. The intended Type C price was £1196, and some cars were released. At least one of them was grafted onto a Tiger a year or so later which, *sans* fins, looked rather good.

In the end, the fate of the Harringtons followed that of the Le Mans racing cars. Rootes decided to drop the coupés in early 1963, after a handful of Type Cs were built. From the enthusiast's standpoint it was a shame. The Harrington Le Mans had a race-proven pedigree, refinement, luxury and styling that outclassed every other popularly priced fastback designed in its wake—both add-on rigs like the Dové GTR4, and factory jobs like the MGB GT. It will be remembered.

Yet more uncommon than the Harrington was the Venezia, which appeared in 1963 under the aegis of Carrozzeria Touring. The Milan firm built this closed Sunbeam along with Alpines and other Rootes products under licence. The Venezia, a sleek 2+2, used Humber Sceptre componentry with a Superleggera aluminium body stretched on a tubular frame. The Sceptre understructure was shipped to Milan and placed in a master jig, where wheel arch pressings and the tubular structure were welded on. The Venezia had a 101in wheelbase and was 11in longer than the Sceptre, giving it a more balanced look. 'The use of the wrap-over Sceptre windscreen has permitted an unusually smooth, slightly domed roof line which contrasts with the flat, angular look of many of the latest small and medium saloon cars,' noted *Autocar*. The waist line is low and there is very little rise over the bonnet at the

base of the screen.' The Venezia was ostensibly a four-seater, though headroom in the rear was marginal. Up front were quad headlamps and a Rapier-style grille. Many niceties—a carpeted boot, twist-knob-controlled quarter lights, thick vinyl upholstery, red door warning lights, amber turn-signal repeaters in the front wings—made it a luxurious tourer.

The Venezia also featured slightly different mechanical details. Its camshaft was a new type, engineered for smoothness, which combined with standard overdrive and 4.22:1 rear axle ratio to give 95mph maximum. It used a cast-iron exhaust manifold with two outlets instead of the single outlet used on early production models. The inlet manifold was supported by two braces, to reduce vibration and contribute to smoothness.

The Venezia was a distinctive car, but expensive: an Italian paid 2.5 million lire (about £1400) for one. Few were built, and most were confined to the local market.

Alongside the Venezia, Touring also manufactured Italian-market Alpines, and it was noticed that they were finless, thus better looking, especially as the tailfin was becoming an anachronism. A finless Alpine would appear in England, but not quite yet; in the meantime, Rootes were releasing the finned Series III, in two versions: sports car and 'GT'.

The smart facia and instrument layout of the Sunbeam Venezia, which retained all the dials and controls of a normal Sunbeam of the period, though assembled in Italy

Changes common to all Series III Alpines were to the good, Rootes again responding to criticisms gleaned from owners and the press. A new hardtop design appeared, more graceful, more streamlined and with better visibility and improved ventilation via pivoting quarter lights behind the door glass. The only criticism of the new top was that the 'glass' was plastic, and subject to crazing. The fixed quarter lights already fitted to Italian Alpines were applied to Series IIIs, and the number plate location was relocated to below the rear bumper.

Drastic improvements occurred inside. Microcell bucket seats with ample side support replaced the relatively flat Series I/II buckets, and were adjustable for rake with locking levers at the hinge points. *Road & Track* noted that the new Alpines would fit 'anyone from the Cardiff Giant to J. Fred Muggs', and wasn't far wrong: in addition to fore/aft/rake, the seats could be adjusted for height and for cushion tilt; the steering wheel had a $2\frac{1}{2}$in telescoping feature and even the pedals had a choice of positions for long and short leg reach. There were 64 different combinations all told. Also standard for the first time on Alpine IIIs were two-speed windscreen wipers, screenwash, headlight flasher switch and 'Day-glo' coloured needles for the instruments. The soft top was redesigned for easier operation, the separate cantrails being eliminated.

In the new Sunbeams, Rootes solved the traditional sports car problem of inadequate luggage space. Twin 6.75 gallon fuel tanks were placed in the rear wings, interconnected with a single filler, and the spare tyre was mounted upright at the front of the boot. This gave a relatively enormous 11cu ft luggage capacity—more than any other sports car.

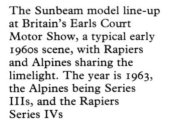

The Sunbeam model line-up at Britain's Earls Court Motor Show, a typical early 1960s scene, with Rapiers and Alpines sharing the limelight. The year is 1963, the Alpines being Series IIIs, and the Rapiers Series IVs

The mechanical spec of the Alpine convertible, now called Sports Tourer, was identical to that of the Series II, except for closer ratio gears, which eliminated the awkward pause between first and second, and larger disc brakes. The GT model, however, was detuned for the sake of smoothness and quiet. It used Zenith W1A3 carbs instead of W1P3s, and a large air filter/silencer instead of individual 'gravel screen' air cleaners. It also employed the Venezia's two-branch cast-iron exhaust manifold, rather than the welded, extractor type. This provided only 80.3bhp, and 3 less pounds-feet of torque. The GT was thus slower off the line, though top speed wasn't affected.

GTs came as standard with the new hardtop (which was an option on the convertible), and were not fitted with soft tops, though their hardtops could be removed. Whilst this may sound strange to English ears, California often goes several weeks without rain. Deleting the soft top also allowed Rootes to nicely upholster the rear compartment, and even add a couple of highly occasional 'seats'. GTs differed from convertibles by having a walnut appliqué facia and wood-rimmed steering wheel. Most remarkable, both Series IIIs were cheaper than the Series II, by £86 to £145.

The GT was obviously aimed at the American market and priced to sell. There was a serious reason for this. Rootes were

Compare this interior shot of a Series V Alpine with that of the Tiger—the only real difference is the shape of the gearbox tunnel, and the position of the gear lever

New York backdrop shows off this Mark IV in 1964. Rootes Motors Inc. stated that this model was a 'Grand Turismo with detachable hardtop, and deep pile carpeting'. No mention was made of its performance. Probably just as well—it was hailed as the first imported sports car with automatic transmission

hurting by 1963, more than most outsiders thought. Lord William's first crucial mistake had been made in 1961, when he allowed the British government to talk him into expanding to Linwood, Renfrewshire, Scotland. This was really his only option, if he cared to expand at all. The government wanted to encourage industry in depressed areas, and refused to grant Rootes permission to expand their capacity in Coventry. Similar policies also caused the opening of BMC and Triumph works in places like South Wales, Merseyside and Scotland, all of which came to grief. In these far-flung locations, they were faced with a workforce unused to the monotony of a car plant, required to institute ground-up training programmes, and would eventually experience poor labour relations. Rootes had simultaneously accepted a large government loan, with heavy interest. When the market for cars softened, the annual splash of black ink suddenly turned red. More trouble arrived in the form of a lengthy and bitter wage dispute at the British & Light Steel Pressings works in Acton, which produced not only Humber shells but Rapier and Alpine bodies as well. Supplies of Alpines to the vital North American market began drying up—at precisely the time Rootes were trumpeting their Le Mans triumphs. There were plenty of customers, but no cars to sell to them.

Linwood became operational in 1962, and began producing Hillman Imps in the spring of 1963, but the Imp was a monumental fiasco, uncompetitive and subject to reliability problems. All told, the events of 1961–63 did not bode well for the hitherto successful Rootes dynasty. It was at this time that the company renewed their search for a merger partner, culminating in the sale of 30 per cent of voting shares and 50 per cent of non-voting shares to Chrysler in June 1964.

Lord Rootes was relieved of the burden of watching the demise of his empire. He died in December 1964, widely mourned by Coventry, whose interests he had served so well. His title passed to Geoffrey Rootes, who had already become managing director of the car group; he became deputy chairman under Sir Reginald in 1965, and chairman in 1967.

Lord Rootes had personally instituted the Chrysler deal, and he had great hopes for it in 1964. In that year, we must remember, it looked as though he'd made a wise decision. Chrysler was prosperous, highly profitable and needed entry to the European Economic Community. So indeed did Ryton. It appeared to everyone that Britain's entry, with her EFTA partners, was imminent. No one predicted the stumbling block personified by President de Gaulle, and Chrysler's decline was yet a decade away.

Chrysler became majority owner in 1967, and Rootes became Chrysler United Kingdom in 1970. Vast rationalization then set in: Singer vanished, and Humber became a mere badge-engineered Hillman. It wasn't until the mid-seventies that the desperate plight of the operation was revealed, by dint of which Chrysler-UK was sold to Peugeot-Citroën.

Back in America, Chrysler joyously announced the availability of Rootes franchises to its dealer network, and Rootes helped out early in 1964 by introducing a restyled Series IV Alpine. The new model was shorn at last of its controversial tailfins—ironic in a way, for it was Chrysler which inspired them. A new, single-bar grille

World Champion Grand Prix driver Jack Brabham marketed a series of engine tune-up kits for Alpines and Rapiers in the early 1960s. This shot was posed in 1965, for the Alpine is a Series V model; the single seater is, of course, a Repco-Brabham

carrying the old Talbot lion in its centre was installed, together with thin bumper guards with rubber buffer strips front and rear. Detail touches included a Vinyl-covered facia for the open Alpine and tiny 'eyelids' for the facia warning lights, to dim them at night —a clever idea that was a Rootes exclusive.

Attempting to widen the Alpine market still further, the Series IV offered the option of automatic transmission. The unit was supplied by Borg-Warner: a three-speed, fully automatic box, with PRNDL-stick sprouting from a floor location. Rootes-New York claimed one driver achieved 0–60 in 12.6 seconds with the automatic, but on average it was more like 15 seconds.

The difference in specification between Series III models was now erased, through a compromise. For both cars, Rootes used a 'replica of the branched manifold in cast iron', as *Autocar* put it. Instead of twin Zeniths, a compound Solex carb was used. This provided 87.5bhp (gross) at 5000rpm for both models—five more hp for the GT, four less for the convertible.

Other Series IV changes included the elimination of grease points through the use of nylon or sealed joints, and a doubled (6000-mile) oil change interval through the use of a new filter. Spring and shock settings were modified slightly to improve the ride: this caused increased understeer, though on the apex of fast bends there was a slow transition to near neutral steer.

Finally, in the autumn of 1964, one last step towards perfection arrived—all-synchromesh manual transmission. There was no change in gear ratios, but 'synchro-first' provided the Alpine with that final bit of flexibility and a thoroughly modern specification.

There was still more left in the old warhorse, though: the Series V, the last of the line, was announced in 1965. And it was the best Alpine yet.

The most interesting aspect of this version was its engine: larger in capacity at 1725cc, yet no larger in dimension, since the increase was made by enlarging the stroke. There were now five bearings instead of three, with all that implied for strength and longevity. The five mains alone would make Series Vs the most sought-after Alpines among latterday collectors. An aluminium sports-type head with more efficient porting was common to both Rapier and Alpine, and the single Solex carb was replaced with twin Stromberg CDs. A finned-pipe oil cooler was standard, and the electrical system switched to negative earth.

This was easily the quickest Alpine yet, especially with overdrive and the 4.22:1 rear axle ratio that came with it. It offered for the first time a genuine 100mph capability, and would accelerate alongside an MGB without losing ground—also for the first time. The Series V was the complete, the ultimate Sunbeam Alpine— the fastest, most comfortable and most refined. Yet, remarkably, through a decade of evolution, its price had increased just £40 in England and *decreased* (by $1) in the USA!

A number of minor details should be noted. For the first time on

RAPIER
SPORTS SALOON

A thrilling sports saloon, with an exciting specification, furnished and equipped to luxury standards.
The proved 1,725 c.c. engine gives powerful, flexible performance, swift acceleration in all gears, power for long climbs and sustained cruising, with top speeds over 95 m.p.h. A rally-bred Sunbeam!
Some Rapier features. Powerful 1,725 c.c. o.h.v. engine :: 5-bearing crankshaft, compound carburettor, aluminium cylinder head :: 35-amp alternator :: Sports-type, 4-speed, all-synchromesh gearbox :: Servo-assisted braking, front disc brakes :: Fully adjustable front seats, adjustable steering wheel :: Full instrumentation, heating/ventilation system :: No greasing points :: Overdrive an optional extra.

COLOUR SCHEMES
Single tone.
Royal Blue Metallic with Grey upholstery.
Laurel Green Metallic with Green upholstery.
Two tones.
The first-named colour is the predominant body colour and the second is the roof and side flash.
Autumn Gold Metallic/Embassy Black with Black upholstery.
Silver Grey Metallic/Embassy Black with Black upholstery.
The first-named colour is the predominant body colour and the second is the side flash only.
Sherwood Green Metallic/Embassy Black with Black upholstery.
Silver Grey Metallic/Pippin Red with Red upholstery.
Pippin Red/Embassy Black with Black upholstery.
Lagoon Blue Metallic/Embassy Black with Black upholstery.

ALPINE
GRAN TURISMO HARDTOP

This magnificent Alpine has an elegant, detachable hard top and other exclusive features. The hard top is light and easy to handle. It locks in position, as illustrated, to form weather-tight coachwork. It can be quickly unlocked and detached, converting the car to an open tourer. Refinements include a large backlight and quarter-light ventilators.

Sporting performance with touring luxury

The latest Alpine models have many new refinements. The brilliant 1,725 c.c. Sunbeam engine gives swift acceleration, smooth and flexible performance, with road speeds up to 100 m.p.h. Road-holding is masterly.
Overdrive is an optional extra.
Some Alpine features. Twin carburettors :: Aluminium cylinder head, 5-bearing crankshaft, 35-amp alternator :: 4-speed all-synchromesh gearbox :: Servo-assisted braking, with front disc brakes :: Adjustable steering wheel, sportsman's instrument panel, rally-type controls, padded grab rail :: Footwell ventilators :: No greasing points

COLOUR SCHEMES
Carnival Red with Black upholstery.
Commodore Blue with Black upholstery.
Polar White with Black upholstery.
Polar White with Red upholstery.
British Racing Green with Black upholstery.
Orchid Green with Black upholstery.
Mediterranean Blue with Black upholstery.
All Soft Tops are Black.
G.T. models have Hard Tops in matching body colour.
Hard Tops are also available in Black if ordered as a special accessory.

ALPINE
SPORTS TOURER

The classic Sunbeam - a stylish 'convertible' that can be used as an open tourer or weather-tight saloon. The hood assembly is tight and snug-fitting. The hood can be quickly raised or lowered and concealed inside the bodywork - a new stowage cover facilitates this operation. Wrap-around front screen and efficient draught sealing. Additional hard top at extra cost.

Sunbeam quality and high-precision engineering

One of the last brochures featuring the Alpine obviously came with Chrysler influence. Series V 1725 version only boasts a top speed of 95mph. Too slow by half

the Series V, interior cockpit ventilation was adequate: there were air vents on each side of the facia. The rear brakes were not discs, as one magazine had predicted, but they were now self-adjusting. The folded-down soft top was now covered by a snap-on fabric apron—less neat than the folding metal panels, but less prone to damaging the material.

Road & Track summed up the case for Ryton in their road test of March 1966. They liked the enormous boot, which accepted 26in suitcases; they liked the all-synchro gearbox, the good brakes, the smooth ride and pleasantly sporty performance. They liked the space behind the seats, and they especially liked the fuel consumption—30mpg (24 Imperial) despite a non-overdrive model fitted with the lower (4.22) axle ratio. The only complaint they had was that the roadster didn't come with sun visors. (They were optional.) 'To sum it up we can think of nothing more appropriate to say than that the Alpine V has retained the virtues of the previous versions and added a few new ones, which assure that it continues to be one of the most civilized of the contemporary sports cars.'

Continue it did. This best of all Alpines stayed in production

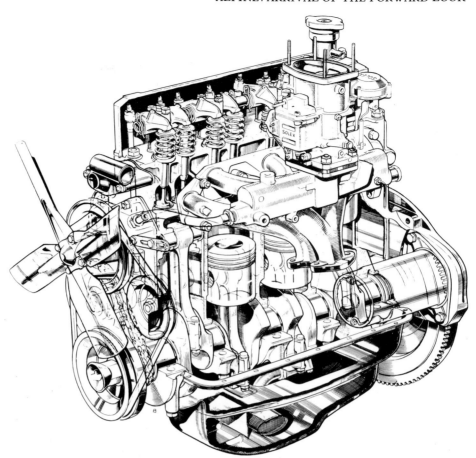

Along came the 1725 engine for the then-uprated Series V Alpine. What's obvious from this drawing is that the Rootes Group were trying hard—there's a sort of a tubular freeflow manifold but it's defeated by the compound Solex. The last Alpine series is probably the best, though

until the end of January 1968, and some were actually titled as 1969 models in the US. Why did it stop? American safety regulations put an end to fuel-tanks-in-rear-wings, and later the headlamp height wouldn't have satisfied Washington. There were also the continuing late-sixties production problems of Rootes, which kept the supply of Alpines uneven—anathema to American dealers used to unending supplies and on-the-spot deliveries.

Even so, the basic Sunbeam Alpine had lasted a solid decade—longer than most sports cars, longer by far than any of its permutations, the Harringtons, the GTs, the Tiger. It outlasted and outsold them all. It proved itself respectable, if not invincible, in competition, and at Le Mans it made history. Above all, it provided good value for money. And it still does: an Alpine is about the least expensive two-seater on today's collector market, and at the $2500 or £1000 it takes to own a good one, it's more tempting now than ever. Through five generations, Rootes had rendered something increasingly rare in the automotive field: an honest car which always gave, as the Studebaker brothers used to say, a little more than its makers promised.

7

Tiger: The glorious mistake

Unless motoring writers do something to prevent it, the Sunbeam Tiger is in danger of becoming another Edsel, glorified out of all proportion to its net worth and industrial significance. It is a popular car these days—at last. Clubs have been formed, books have been written, the Tiger has been dissected and categorized by a host of cheering fans. But some noises now sounding from Tigerland border on hagiolatry.

It is necessary to set the Tiger in its place, which is not to denigrate it as a motorcar. Historians (if we are historians, which I doubt) are obliged to paint accurate pictures. To do so, Wilson McComb once wrote, 'We may sometimes have to challenge a few statements that other people accept without question. [We must not] get too misty eyed and sentimental about the girls *or* the cars. We must ask ourselves if they were really that good.'

Was the Tiger really that good? Was it a thoroughbred that causes people who should know better to say that it takes up to $15,000 to buy one? The answer is at best equivocal. I am mildly qualified to say this. I was among the 7000-odd souls (and to many we *were* odd) who bought a Sunbeam Tiger new.

Confessions first. My 1966 Mark I still heads the long list of Cars I Should Have Never Sold. Midnight blue with matching hardtop, fitted with one of the better-grained walnut dashboards (they varied), it was the most soul-satisfying two-seater I ever owned. It was ideal for America, where the determined driver may cover 800 miles in a day on string-straight freeways. Its effortless performance, relative luxury, quiet and comfort cost the grand total of $3800, about £1360 at the time—which today would buy you exactly one-half of a Polski-Fiat. It cost $100 more than the noisy, hard-riding, vastly overrated Austin-Healey 3000; $1700 less than the sports car world's *beau ideal*, the Jaguar E type; and some $7000 less than the nearest 'Anglo-American sports bastard', the ugly Jensen C-V8.

I traded my Tiger in after 25,000 miles, receiving $2500 towards an air-conditioned Karmann Ghia. Yes, I know—but the Ghia made practical sense on the long, hot business trips I was then

This photograph was published by something called the Simca-Rootes News Bureau (Chrysler's way of telling the American market that they had a foothold in Europe). This Sunbeam Tiger was to have 'speeds to 150 miles an hour' —wishful thinking. Standard American specification Tiger

condemned to endure. The Tiger, however, was unforgettable. And as its stature rose in retrospect, it became *more* unforgettable. I will own another one some day.

Objective industry observers must, however, label the Tiger a failure, partly due to its own deficiencies as a product, partly due to outside factors. It was *not* a hot seller, no matter what the cacophony says; I've talked to dealers who were flogging leftover Tigers at cost in order to get rid of them. Had things been otherwise, the wealthy corporation that was Chrysler in 1967 would have kept the Tiger in production—by hook or by crook.

In Rootes showrooms the Tiger suffered from the converse of what I call 'the Kaiser complex'. American buyers in 1954 wouldn't touch a Kaiser Manhattan that cost the same as a Pontiac, even if it was supercharged and would stay with many V8s, because all they saw under the bonnet were six lonely cylinders. Conversely the Tiger was an anomaly in showrooms laden with Hillmans (Hillmen?), Singers, Humbers, even Alpines. It also looked far too much like the cheaper Alpine, which would have been anathema to a Detroit product planner. Unique styling is vital in a car like this. It is, for example, the one thing standing between that rolling juggernaut the 1981 Corvette and a sales catastrophe.

The Corvette makes an interesting comparison, in its Tiger-era form—which wasn't bad. In 1965, you could buy a Sting Ray for only $300 more than a Sunbeam Tiger, and a lot of Americans did —24,000 of them. If any of these considered the Tiger it would have been remarkable—although on paper, the Tiger should have competed at least mildly with the Corvette. The Tiger lacked that essential visibility which made the Sting Ray (and the E type)

Apart from the badging, and the discreet chrome strip along each flank, there was virtually nothing external to identify a Sunbeam Tiger from a Sunbeam Alpine. This car had the optional detachable hardtop

successful in the vital American market. And, from the opposite end of the scale, to MG and Triumph folk who might have moved up to it, the Tiger lacked pedigree. No one in America had forgotten the heritage of the Sunbeam marque. To us Yanks, it never existed.

What all these factors led to is well known. After a half-hearted attempt to stuff in a Valiant V8 as alternative to the hated ford (lower case, please), Chrysler simply dumped the Tiger. Pay no attention to the intriguing, well-known photos of 'future' designs: they are meaningless, trifles light as air. No Chrysler executive ever came close to commissioning a production prototype. The Tiger died because it didn't sell.

This now recorded, we can turn to a review of the Tiger *qua* car with lighter hearts, having done our duty by history.

It was a good, even brilliant idea when it dawned on the fertile mind of young Ian Garrad, Lewis's brother, then West Coast manager for Rootes Motors Inc., the USA subsidiary. Ian was not, however, the first to think of transforming the Alpine by an infusion of horsepower. The company had already considered, in this approximate order, a Humber Hawk 2.3-litre four, a dohc Alfa 1.6 four, a Daimler 2.5 V8 and a Ferrari engine (probably the 1.9-litre dohc V6 then under development, which eventually found its way into the Dino). The Humber 2.3, in a higher state of tune, might have coped, but was heavy and unmodern. The Alfa engine wasn't available. Enzo Ferrari backed out of a promising deal to supply Alpine-Ferraris in 1962. The lovely little Daimler 2.5 would have been ideal, and more presentable in an Alpine than in the ugly SP250, but it had dimensional problems. Ian Garrad knew about most of these false starts, and it hurt. When Ian's personal, highly tuned Alpine was outdragged one day by the proverbial little old lady ('She never saw me and wasn't even trying to outrun me'), he decided to pursue an engine transplant in earnest.

Jack Brabham, who with Stirling Moss did wondrous things with Alpines at Riverside's Times Grand Prix in October 1962,

* Ian Garrad's quotes from Gregory Wells's article, 'Sunbeam Tiger, A Bloomin' Quick Hybrid', *Special-Interest Autos*, April 1981, with permission of author and publishers.

told Ian where to look: the stuffer ought to be an American V8. This would provide gobs of torque, effortless acceleration and high-speed stamina, yet it was simple in concept and probably available from a Detroit manufacturer. If there is one thing we Americans built well, it was the V8 engine, and 'Blackie' knew it. Alas, not everyone back in Ryton agreed with him. Said Brabham to author Mike Taylor, 'They were listening but seemed embarrassed at the idea of an American engine in one of their cars.'

The undaunted Garrad nevertheless set his service manager Walt McKenzie to measuring the Alpine engine compartment with a yardstick, thence to local dealerships to measure potential V8s. He thought the 3.5-litre Buick-Olds V8 might do the job, but it proved too big. The measuring produced a substitute that would easily adapt: the Ford Fairlane smallblock V8, with 4.2 litres (260cu in).

Nothing in the cockpit gives away the secret of the Tiger's 4.2-litre engine, and that was one of the many marketing problems of selling such a fast car

Ford engineer Robert Stirrat had conceived of this watershed powerplant—light, efficient, with plenty of latitude for high-performance modifications. Advanced thin-wall casting techniques made it the lightest cast-iron V8 on the world market. It was a short-stroke design, with full-length, full-circle water jackets;

The American Ford V8
engine, in spite of its 4.2-
litre displacement, was
surprisingly compact

high-turbulence, wedge-shaped combustion chambers; hydraulic
valve lifters and centrifugal vacuum advance distributor. When
first produced for the 1962 Ford Fairlane it displaced 3.6 litres
and offered 145hp; in 1963 the 4.2 was made optional, its two-
barrel Ford carburettor helping it achieve 164bhp at 4400rpm. As
Carroll Shelby was soon to prove with his Cobra, this modestly
tuned engine had enormous potential—better than 1bhp per
cubic inch.

Because of Shelby's vast experience and close ties to Ford, he
seemed the obvious man to assemble a running prototype, which
was essential. Garrad knew there was no point in simply suggesting
the idea to Ryton. Bill Carroll, west coast editor of *Automotive
News*, promised Ian he would talk to Shelby, but Garrad couldn't
wait; he rang Shelby-American's offices in Venice, California, and
made an appointment. 'Shelby was both co-operative and enthusiastic,' Ian said.

A bonnetful of engine—
squeezing the small-block
Ford V8 of 4.2 litres into the
monocoque of the Sunbeam
Alpine helped to produce the
Sunbeam Tiger

After a conference between Shelby, Garrad, Shelby developmental expert and test driver Ken Miles and Ford's liaison man Ray Geddes, the project was pronounced feasible. Shelby-American offered to build a prototype for $10,000, plus a per-car percentage on any sales resulting from it.

Garrad immediately called John Panks, managing director of Rootes Motors Inc. in New York, the North American headquarters. Here was a car enthusiast—his pride and joy was a 1921 dohc straight-eight Sunbeam. Panks was in Los Angeles in two days. Together, he and Ian Garrad conferred on what they saw as a Corvette rival, and a club with which to hammer rival MG and Triumph. They named it, after a thirties land-speed-record car, the Sunbeam 'Thunderbolt'.

Next step: an approach to higher authority. In February 1963, export manager Brian Rootes came to San Francisco for a dealer conference, where Ian offered to buy him a few drinks. 'I particularly remember this episode,' Ian said, 'as the programme involved a heavy elbow exercise (starting at seven the previous evening) and the wipe-out of four other executives at 2am, finally giving me a chance to speak to Brian quietly about—to British eyes—my outrageous proposal.' By 4am, 'with the able assistance of a certain Mr Cognac', approval was near. Said Brian Rootes, 'It's a bloody good idea.' The two parted. Ian was in bed at 5.30am when the phone rang. 'Do you really think Carroll Shelby can do it?', asked Brian Rootes. Ian said Shelby could. Brian replied, 'At that price, when can he start? But for God's sake, keep it quiet from Dad until you hear from me. I'll work the $10,000 out some way.' The money was liberated from Rootes-North America's advertising account.

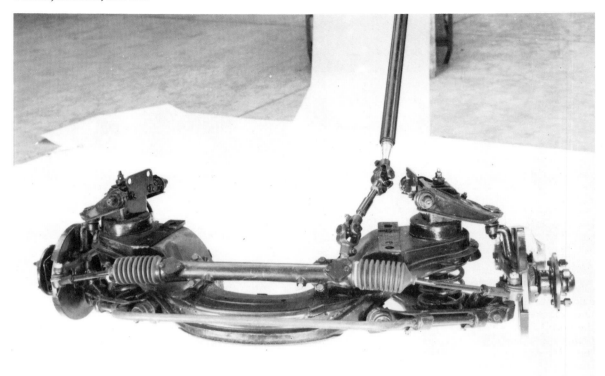

This solid and sturdy front suspension sub-assembly found its way on to Rapiers, Alpines and Tigers in the 1950s and 1960s. The rack and pinion steering, in this case, identifies the application as that of the V8-engined Tiger

The much more robust back axle of the Tiger helped to tame the massive torque of the Ford V8 engine, and the Panhard rod helped to keep the suspension movement in check

The Sunbeam Tiger at the British Earls Court Motor Show of 1966, with a Series V Alpine behind it, and the latest line in Aston Martins close by. The Tiger's wheels were non-standard

Carroll Shelby had estimated the work would take eight weeks (it eventually took 12), which disappointed Ian Garrad, whose enthusiasm was nearing red-line. Was there an alternative? Well, Ken Miles still had a shop of his own, and he offered to do a quick lash-up in the meantime, for $600. This was too good to pass up, and in March Ian Garrad sent a Series II Alpine to Miles. Ken found a 260 V8, but couldn't locate a manual gearbox and substituted a Ford-O-Matic. Very little calculation was involved—the engine was just dumped in, to the same approximate spot the 1.6-litre had been. The regular fan didn't fit, so Miles installed a pair of small electric fans out of a Jaguar. He added a Sun rev counter, repainted the car candy apple red, and delivered it to Garrad five days after he'd started.

Ian's first ride was memorable. 'It was about midnight, in pouring rain, and there were no windshield wipers. Ken aimed the car up the Golden State Freeway at such a high rate of speed that I can honestly confess to furtively looking for an 'eject' button. The car was literally dangerous, an unpredictable handler.' Miles moved the engine farther back towards the scuttle, and improved the steering with a pirated rack-and-pinion unit. After tearing the hubs out of stock Alpine shells he installed Mini-Lite mags. Garrad tested the Miles car for 5000 miles, and wasn't sure he had a winner. The power was there, but this was not the kind of hot-rod that would melt Lord Rootes' Tory heart.

Happily the Shelby-built car emerged on 29 April 1963, and was much better. Shelby's Phil Remington (project director) and George Boskoff (head mechanic) had carved their way into the firewall, pushing the V8 as far back as it could possibly go, then strengthening the scuttle to make up for lost support. They replaced the Alpine steering box with an MGA rack-and-pinion unit

DOWN, CATS
HERE COMES THE REAL TIGER

There are a lot of cats roaming around beating their chests. But it takes a real cat to recognize the top cat—The Tiger—a supremely masculine, true British sports car with a wallop that makes lesser cars sulk in their garages. Fast? With a Ford V-8 power plant it doesn't take off, it leaps! That's why it placed first and second in its class in the 1965 Monte Carlo Rally. It takes a lot of know-how to produce the world's fastest sports car for $3499. And it takes a lot of man to ride this Tiger. Test yourself in the Sunbeam Tiger today. **P.S.** Look at the Tiger's lair-mate, the Sunbeam Alpine (SCCA Class F champion), priced at an easy-to-take **$2399**. *ASK ABOUT OUR OVERSEAS DELIVERY PLAN*

"CAR & DRIVER" READERS VOTE THE TIGER BEST GRAND TOURING SPORTS CAR $2500 TO $3500

'65 Sunbeam Tiger
A ROOTES PRODUCT **SUNBEAM**

Prices East P. O. E. Whitewall tires optional extra. For information write Rootes Motors, 505 Park Avenue, N.Y. or 9830 West Pico Blvd., Los Angeles

Art Arfons...world's fastest man on wheels... owns the world's fastest sports car for $3499*

Britain contributed the racing chassis. America provided the mighty Ford V-8 power plant. The men in England who build the famed Sunbeam sports cars put chassis and engine together to create the hottest car to hit 1965. Test the Tiger's cat-quick reflexes. Touch the throttle and get the ride of your life.

'65 Sunbeam Tiger *A ROOTES PRODUCT* **SUNBEAM**

Rootes Motors advertised the Tiger aggressively in North America. They tried several tacks—two were those of emphasising the car's name and associating the car with someone successful in motor sport

mounted ahead of the front axle. There was no space for the stock Ford oil filter or fuel pump; the latter was replaced by a Smiths electric pump mounted in the Alpine's battery box behind the offside front seat. The battery was relocated to the boot, the spare tyre laid flat and both items covered by a floorboard. Boskoff also installed a cut-down Ford radiator, a beefy front anti-sway bar, an electric rev counter and revised the spring rates. Doane Spencer of Hollywood Sports Cars in Los Angeles—who'd been one of the first to recommend the thinwall Ford V8—helped by adapting a Studebaker Lark final drive to replace the oversized Ford Galaxie unit.

Everyone involved admits how much better the Tiger II was. 4.7 litre Ford V8, 13 inch wheels and four-wheel disc brakes were all mooted. This is one of a few IIs made—note egg box grille, painted headlamp trims and changed lettering. Major Tiger problem was that it looked like the Alpine

Official photo caption reads 'The Tiger II, currently a limited-edition model of the Tiger I for high performance enthusiasts, incorporates significant additions and refinements'. April 1, 1967

Ken Miles took the white Shelby car to Riverside, through downtown Los Angeles and across the Mojave Desert—refining, perfecting, erasing the weak spots. Then Ian Garrad spent nearly 40,000 miles behind the wheel. And eventually he was satisfied.

The story of the down-and-up UK reception of Ian Garrad and 'Thunderbolt' is well known. From a fixed appointment with Lord Rootes he was bumped to assistant chief engineer Peter Ware, who was too busy, leaving Ian with assistant-to-the-assistant Peter

Wilson. After a mind-blowing ride, Wilson jumped for a phone and Ian climbed back up the ladder. Lord Rootes came back smiling from his own test drive, even though his-usually-limousine-borne-Lordship had left the handbrake on, and the smell of burning brake linings enveloped Ryton-on-Dunsmore. Lord Rootes sought out Henry Ford II, finding him stripped for sun in his favoured Bahamas. Henry promised 3600 4.2-litre V8s per year if Ford president Lee Iacocca would approve. After being convinced that Rootes offered no direct competition to his forthcoming Mustang, Iacocca lent his co-operation.

Lord Rootes also made two crucial product decisions, which would have been better left to the professionals. These have received insufficient emphasis in accounts of why the Tiger failed. First, he decreed that the production car should not differ appreciably from the Alpine. Second, just after its introduction at the New York Auto Show in spring 1964, he accepted John Panks's suggestion to name it 'Tiger'. This was in honour of Sir Henry Segrave's Coatalen-designed Sunbeam V12 Land Speed Record car, which held the mark in 1926 at 152.33mph.

The second decision was one of necessity. Chrysler, it was found, already owned the rights to 'Thunderbolt'. The name 'Tiger' was also claimed, by Leyland for a truck, but the latter agreed to Rootes' use of it on a car.

Lord William had made many wise decisions in his long career, but these weren't among them. Perhaps because he was getting on in years, his usual acute sense of American values deserted him. He failed to realize that few in the States had ever heard of Segrave or Coatalen, let alone their car; more important, he failed to appreciate the advantages of distinctive styling. The 'Alpine look', fine enough intrinsically, was to prove a major Tiger sales problem.

Though Thrupp & Maberly might have handled the Tiger's specialized construction, they didn't have the capacity for 3600 cars a year, nor the expertise for production development. Rootes itself was cramped, so management turned to Jensen Motors of West Bromwich, Birmingham, to finalise the car and then mass-produce it. The product development team included Jensen chief engineer Kevin Beattie and his assistant Mike Jones (both former Rootesmen), Jensen chief design engineer Eric Neale; Rootes' brilliant Alec Caine as overall project engineer; and Rootes development engineer Don Tarbun. The team worked not at Jensen but at the old Humber experimental department at the Stoke, Coventry works.

Although Tarbun in particular considered the Shelby prototype crude, its concept was sound and few developmental problems were encountered. They had to design a flat, dry-element air cleaner; adjust the shock settings and throttle linkage; come up with an adequate radiator; and cure the prototype's severe axle tramp. The latter was handled partly by a Panhard rod and special Salisbury rear axle, and partly by Traction Master anti-tramp bars,

Photographed in front of some railings almost certainly in New York, this unadorned Tiger prototype was probably the best looking. Although a mistake for the Rootes Group, the concept and some of the execution was right. Pity

which were first optional, later standard. Jensen designed the dual exhaust system. The team selected a tall 2.88:1 final drive ratio for tractability at speed and insurance against over-revving—the 4.2 was apt to blow up over 5000rpm. Rootes durability tests followed, and in all Jensen built 14 prototypes. (See appendix.)

Product planning gaffes continued to occur. The 'Alpine-clone' concept had dictated two Tigers, corresponding to the two Alpines: a GT with walnut dash, and a vinyl-dash roadster. Eventually they switched to a single model, with standard walnut dash and optional hardtop. But why they didn't pursue a coupé version with, perhaps, the Harrington Type C hardtop (at least one such Tiger was made) is not recorded. The most minimal market research would have shown that out of the 25,000 to 30,000 Corvettes being sold per year, 30 to 40 per cent of them were fixed-head models. A 'Harrington Tiger' would have helped, not hindered, and cost little.

When Jensen prototype AF8 (for 'Alpine Ford') arrived in New York for its April auto show debut, it was probably the dullest looking V8 sports car ever minted. Except for understated '260' badging and dual exhausts, it was an exact Alpine replica. Panks and Garrad called a panic meeting after the debut, although it was too late to do anything of real substance. They managed to put a thin stainless steel strip on the bodysides, improving it visually. Their efforts to install an egg-crate grille came to naught, although this was used on the later Tiger II. It was just as well the latter didn't make it, for it had no styling relationship with the car and frankly looked awful.

A 'Sunbeam 260' displayed at Turin in October 1964 had a clear plastic panel in the bonnet, which made the V8's presence readily apparent—but this was hardly something for production. Thus the Tiger went on sale, its fate virtually sealed.

Production Sunbeam Tigers were very fully equipped, per Rootes tradition. The plan to offer wire wheels failed because the

The prototype Le Mans Sunbeam Tiger, as built for Rootes by Brian Lister's workshops in Cambridge

The Le Mans Tigers were later developed into formidable British-circuit machines. Rootes employee John Harris (who was also a respected Healey racing test driver) on yet another development run

Jimmy Blumer at the wheel of the second Le Mans Tiger in the 1964 Le Mans 24 Hour race. The car broke its crankshaft, due to faulty engine preparation by a supplier

spokes couldn't take the performance stress. All Tigers came with ordinary disc wheels, Alpine hub caps and tatty looking trim surrounds. This left a very basic option list: radio, heater, white-wall tyres and hardtop. (The latter was ostensibly available in 'body colour', but in practice most were delivered in white or black. I had to wait a week while my dealer rendered a white hardtop Midnight blue. Since it wasn't painted at the same time as the car, the colours never quite matched.) The interior was a nice blend of Alpine IV upholstery with extra thick pile carpets, but the walnut dash still lacked a cover for the glovebox.

In August 1965 what was called the 'Mark Ia' Tiger began production. Though the Ia used different serial numbers due to computerization by Rootes, they were mainly unchanged from Mark Is. They did benefit from the Alpine V's new soft-vinyl hood storage boot, cockpit ventilators and embossed door panels.

Racing driver Chris Amon was an early Tiger customer, passing up much more esoteric options, including an Iso Rivolta. He summed up the pros and cons for Eoin Young in *Autocar*: 'I bought a Tiger because it seemed to me to combine a simple engine with a lot of reliable horsepower, good performance and a general lack of fussiness in a car that was pleasant looking and comfortable. I think the car handles reasonably well. A lot of people tell me that it doesn't, but I must say that it goes round a corner as fast as I want to go without any problems. The braking is good. It stops in a straight line and stops from high speed well without any fade . . . the Tiger cruises pleasantly between 90 and 100mph. It gets up there quickly and is completely effortless.' Amon's only complaints were the lack of a cigarette lighter and sun visors, both of which were available from Rootes accessory bins.

Stock Tiger performance ranged in the neighbourhood of 120mph, with 0–60 in 8.5 to 9.5 seconds, depending on the individual car. Fuel consumption averaged around 17 (Imp.) to the gallon, though I often achieved 21–22mpg on trips. Obviously the 2.88 axle ratio helped conserve petrol, as well as making high-speed cruising smooth and quiet. But not quiet enough for some.

While most motoring magazines praised the Tiger, Britain's iconoclastic *CAR* opened fire with heavy artillery, condemning it as the Alpine was condemned by calling it 'more of a grand tourer than a sports car'. GTs, George Bishop wrote, 'need to be quiet and well-sprung . . . on the less than brilliant roads of Europe, the Tiger's unsophisticated suspension let it down . . .) as a gentleman's tourer the main thing against the Tiger is its price, and the noise and discomfort which discourage its use in the way for which it is presumably intended.' Most drivers didn't feel that way about their Tigers—but most of them didn't normally travel at 80–90mph, especially in North America.

Bishop had a point about price-competitiveness. The Tiger looked a fair bargain in England at £300 less than a Jaguar; but in the States, Corvette was only $300 away, and the sporty compacts were $1000 less. Wrote *Special-Interest Autos* editor Dave Brownell, a Rootes salesman at the time: 'As a traffic builder the Tiger was a hard ticket to match. Trouble was, about all it did was bring in traffic. It didn't sell in any numbers worth mentioning . . . $4000 was a lot of money for any car in 1964, especially when another Ford V8-powered sporty car called Mustang could be had for under three grand.' (Ford sold over half a million Mustangs in their first year.)

These points are what this writer, and 7000-odd others, chose to ignore. It must be observed that we were of a character devoted to

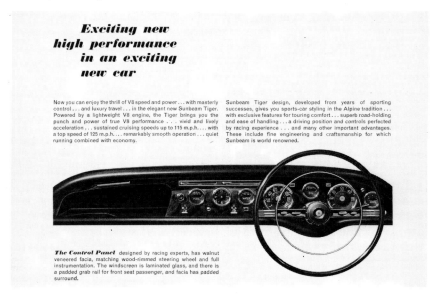

Exciting new high performance in an exciting new car

Now you can enjoy the thrill of V8 speed and power . . . with masterly control . . . and luxury travel . . . in the elegant new Sunbeam Tiger. Powered by a lightweight V8 engine, the Tiger brings you the punch and power of true V8 performance . . . vivid and lively acceleration . . . sustained cruising speeds up to 115 m.p.h. . . . with a top speed of 125 m.p.h. . . . remarkably smooth operation . . . quiet running combined with economy.

Sunbeam Tiger design, developed from years of sporting successes, gives you sports-car styling in the Alpine tradition . . . with exclusive features for touring comfort . . . superb road-holding and ease of handling . . . a driving position and controls perfected by racing experience . . . and many other important advantages. These include fine engineering and craftsmanship for which Sunbeam is world renowned.

The Control Panel designed by racing experts, has walnut veneered facia, matching wood-rimmed steering wheel and full instrumentation. The windscreen is laminated glass, and there is a padded grab rail for front seat passenger, and facia has padded surround.

Taken from the second page of the 'black' Tiger factory brochure Rootes did their best to promote its performance and comfort. Top speed is a quoted 125mph here

the contemporary British sports car concept. We wouldn't have been caught dead in a Mustang, and we *never* waved at Corvettes. While people like us comprised a fair little market, relatively few moved up from MGA or TR3 to a Tiger. Instead they bought a TR4 or MGBGT or Healey, or made the leap to an E type.

If the Tiger disappointed on sales floors, it put the competitions types into a blue funk. The stage was set with the retirement of Norman Garrad as competitions manager in February 1964. He was 64, nearing retirement, but he was also unhappy. 'Rootes wanted to take some of the weight off his shoulders,' Lewis Garrad said, 'which is easy to do, shall we say, in a normal man. But Father, with such tremendous energy, didn't like it at all. He was broken-hearted initially, but he snapped out of it when he was put on special projects he enjoyed. He realized that he didn't want to do all that chasing around.

'I moved off about six months before Dad. I guess I realized that a crisis was coming. The Rootes people were about to be married, and in event of a financial crisis the competitions department would be the first to go. I couldn't see any huge American corporation like Chrysler getting involved in European competitions. The initial Tiger competitions programme was a Garrad programme, though. The first 25 production engines were brought into the competition department and I had to deal with running them for 5000 miles. The cars were quick, but we ran into problems.'

Norman Garrad's replacement was Marcus Chambers, who wondered later why he had come. Just before the 24 Hours of Le Mans in 1964, Chambers actually telephoned Peter Ware to suggest that the cause was hopeless and the Tigers should withdraw. But too much money had been spent, and Ware felt the effort should proceed. It did. Disaster followed.

Peter Harper resting, Ian Hall driving—the 'works' Sunbeam Tiger on the Monte Carlo Rally of 1965

For Le Mans, two racing coupés were built by Lister with steel bodies and Shelby engines. They would have been faster with aluminium bodies as Lister had suggested, but Rootes felt that they should remain as stock as possible. The smooth, Kamm-backed design was by Ron Wisdom of Rootes, and was slippery enough, testing favourably at the MIRA wind tunnel.

The engines were not adequate—it was noted that Shelby recommended the 4.2, while fitting his own racing Cobras with 4.7s. On paper they looked all right, producing 275bhp via twin four-barrel carbs on a custom manifold, with special camshaft, solid lifters and modified heads. But oil pressure failed at 6000rpm, and they overheated with abandon. Handling problems also beset the team, and were never cured. In the race, one Tiger retired with failed pistons after just three hours; the second left with a broken crank at nine hours. Rootes had spent a small fortune on this effort, doubtless remembering the glorious Harrington success in 1961, but the results were so depressing that the works racing effort was scrapped.

Privately entered racing Tigers did better. A Vitafoam-sponsored Targa Florio entry, driven by Peter Harper and the Rev Rupert Jones, won its class in the tough Sicilian road race. Bernard Unett, in a modified Le Mans car with trailing link rear suspension, finished first in class and second overall at both the Freddie Dixon Trophy race and *Autosport* Championship in 1966.

In America, the SCCA placed the Tiger in Class B-Production, with the smaller-engined Corvettes and the (uncompetitive) E types. Carroll Shelby handled preparation of one car at the behest of Ian Garrad, who wished to develop a comprehensive racing programme and 'prodified' spares, knowing the value of racing publicity. The Shelby Tiger had a few moments, including an easy win over E types in its maiden race at Willow Springs, California. But overall it proved disappointing, suffering from skittish handling. For the 1965 season Ian turned to his friend Doane Spencer of Hollywood Sports Cars, who had helped in development of the original prototypes. Fortunes then improved.

Doane went after overheating problems in a major way, shifting components away from the block and cutting-in extractor vents. He adapted cast alloy 7in wheels and mounted disc brakes on the rear wheels. He also wrung 350hp out of the 4.2-litre engine, and the 160mph car won its first Class B race going away. Driver Jim Adams took several more class and overall wins against the hairiest 'production' machinery. Unfortunately he broke a leg in mid-season, and both he and the (somewhat illegal) Tiger were idled. Adams came back in time for the American Road Race of Champions at Daytona and qualified fourth highest, trailing a 427 Cobra and two Shelby GT 350s, but a back-of-the-grid Corvette nailed him on the first lap. The season ended and the Hollywood Tiger was sold off, after Doane Spencer returned the engine to stock.

Alas, 1965 proved flood tide for the Tiger. Doane's 1966 Tiger racing car failed to show promise anywhere, save for a single class win at Riverside. In 1967 SCCA shifted the Tiger to Class C production, which ostensibly should have made it more competitive, but in fact doomed it. The Porsche 911 had arrived, and Porsche literally owned Class C. A series of potent race options (called LAT for 'Los Angeles Tiger'), which included high-rise manifolds, special Holley four-barrel carbs, mag wheels and dual point distributor, were all judged inadmissible by SCCA. Garrad tried the drag-race circuits with success—Tigers were American Hot Rod Association class champion in 1965–67 and NHRA champion in 1965. But the dragstrip crowd was hardly composed of potential Tiger buyers.

On the European rally circuit, high hopes also proved unfounded, as the Tigers had a very uneven career. They won their class in just five major rallies: the Geneva, 1964; the Monte Carlo, 1965; the Scottish, 1965; the Tulip, 1966 and the Acropolis, 1966. Not surprisingly, three of these wins were with Peter Harper up. That was it; the cars proved nose-heavy and subject to poor handling. They had power and stamina, but not the roadholding for the tortuous open roadwork demanded by an increasingly competitive sport.

Though sources differ (see Appendix), at least 572 Mark II Tigers were produced, which varied slightly from the Mark Is. These began production on 10 December 1966, following seven Jensen prototypes and five pre-production models.

As the 4.2-litre smallblock Ford V8 had now been completely superseded by the 4.7 (289cu in.), the latter was used. Remembering the dangers of near-redline revs on the 4.2, stronger valve springs and threaded rocker arms were fitted. The Tiger II redline moved up to 5500rpm. The 4.7-litre developed 200bhp at 4400rpm and nine per cent more torque—282lb ft at 2400rpm. This was the most respected version of the smallblock Ford, as Carroll Shelby had proven, and it was perfect for the Tiger.

Other mechanical changes included a wider-ratio Ford HEH-B four-speed transmission (automatics were considered but dropped due to poor performance and high fuel consumption). The petrol pump was shifted into the old Alpine spare wheel well, an alternator replaced the dynamo and an oil-cooler and Traction Master anti-tramp rods were made standard.

Garrad and Panks were determined to style the Tiger II as differently as possible from the Alpine, realizing the Mark I's definite problem in that regard, and remembering their dis-appointment at the plainness of the 1964 New York show car. They were limited by the fact that no major retooling could be under-taken—due partly to a low budget and partly to the unit body's characteristic resistance to facelifts. Changes were all of the bolt-on or stick-on variety. The elegant single-bar grille was replaced with a busy egg-crate affair, the peaked headlamp rims were blunted and the wheels were painted silver. The neat stainless steel side mould-ing was dropped in favour of stick-on racing stripes and bright metal wheel arch/sill mouldings. The overall effect was to tart-up a once-pretty car. It is notable that Mark I/Ia Tigers remain more sought-after by enthusiasts than Mark IIs, despite the latter's relative scarcity.

I asked a Chrysler stylist what the design people might have done, being surprised that Rootes normally heads-up styling department didn't exercise more authority in the Tiger facelift. (They had done wonders, for example, in keeping the prehistoric Rapier body up to date.) 'Racing stripes don't work on this car,' he told me, 'and neither do wheel-well mouldings and blunt headlamp rims. The wheelbase is short to begin with; these things only make the car shorter and taller. There's not much they *could* do to im-prove on the Mark I, short of a cowl-forward facelift. A return to the original three-bar Alpine grille—or no grille at all—would have perhaps provided enough visual impact without destroying the car's elegance.' Past doubt.

Team rally driver Rosemary Smith trying out a prototype Tiger on the banked circuit at the Industry's MIRA proving ground

Rootes did improve the Tiger II on the inside. Like the Mark Ia, it had interior cockpit ventilation, and in addition the steering wheel was raised slightly to give the driver more space, and the seats received a less-buckety but more comfortable treatment.

Road & Track's test of the Tiger II made some good points, which are worth noting here, because they clearly point out the mistakes that had been made. Like most everyone, *R&T* liked the basic package: 'It is a great pleasure to drive a small car that simply has gobs and gobs of power for its size . . . it does everything with almost disdainful ease.' But the Alpine body had begun 'to look dated', and the Tiger II seemed 'a bit upright, the hood [bonnet] a bit short, the windscreen a bit tall, the hips a bit narrow'.

There was plenty of performance, but more of it 'than the Tiger can handle with complete equanimity. There's a multitude of hops and judders in the rear axle if hard starts are attempted, there's more understeer than we like and when pushed really hard the short wheelbase (86.0in.) seems to conspire against keeping it in a straight line. The standard tyres (5.90-13 Dunlop RS5s) limit the performance potential in its as-delivered condition, as demonstrated by the fact that our 200bhp model got through the standing quarter-mile no more quickly than the 164bhp version and that only a relatively modest 68 per cent-g deceleration rate could be achieved in our panic stop from 80mph braking test . . . Optional 5.5in rims are available from the West Coast distributor, and if it were our Tiger we'd fit those along with radial ply tires.'

But Tiger production had already ended when *Road & Track*'s report appeared. The last car, serial B382100633, rolled out of Jensen on 30 June 1967.

During the brief period when Chrysler Corporation considered continuing the Tiger, a few styling sketches were done which indicated how its visual problems might have been handled. Detroit stylists did try the cowl-forward facelift, conceiving of longer wings, a divided blacked-out grille and a pair of low bonnet scoops. Rear-end changes were confined to new tail-lamp lenses. This proposal, though costly, would have dramatically improved the Tiger. Regretfully it was conceived too late; Rootes should have used something like it back in 1964.

Chrysler Design also conceived of a completely new body with elements of the then-current Dodge-Plymouth lines and a very Detroitish instrument panel. But like all 'future Tiger' sketches, this was mere conjecture, and the programme was soon dead. Rootes had tried to give the car life by wedging in the 4.5-litre Valiant V8, but this had failed on the old body; though a redesigned car could have accepted the Valiant engine, the Tiger was written off before any clay model took shape.

How should history regard the Sunbeam Tiger? The Milestone Car Society, which celebrates the outstanding cars of the 1945–67 period, perhaps sum it up best. They rate the Tiger a Milestone car on the grounds that its design, performance, engineering and

Hot Tiger for Peter Harper in the 1966 Tulip Rally. With an uprated engine fitted and improved brakes and suspension, Harper won the GT catagory. Co-driver was a Mr Turvey with whom Peter had intercom for the event

AHP 294B was one of several successful Tiger rally cars developed by the Rootes competitions department, directed by Marcus Chambers, in the 1964–66 period

craftsmanship were all of a high order. In approving its design they are of course approving that of the basic Sunbeam Alpine, almost faultless in its day, which has nothing to do with the fact that an Alpine-like Tiger didn't sell.

It really was, as other scribers said, more grand tourer than sports car. It should have been conceived, promoted and designed as such, and its role in competitions concentrated on long-haul GT races. Surely it was wrong to give up on the Tiger after one disappointing outing at Le Mans. As Bernard Unett proved, the bugs in the Le Mans cars could be and were eradicated.

As a GT, of course, the Tiger had its faults. But it was a brilliant idea and a tremendous value for money. Happily, prices on the collector market still haven't blown through the ceiling. For those of us who appreciated it when new, the Tiger still sings a siren song, and its place in our hearts is secure.

8

Imp: The car that killed the Rootes Group?

Perhaps it was never as simple as all that, and perhaps many other factors were involved, but to a historian it seems clear that the Rootes Group became trapped in financial decline from the day they started building the Imp. Too many 'firsts' almost made this inevitable—it was their first truly small car, their first rear-engined car, and it was also the first Rootes car to be built in Scotland.

Prototypes built in the 1950s were completely different from those built at the start of the 1960s, which in turn differed considerably from the cars actually put on sale in 1963. The original car, nicknamed the 'Slug', was not even an official project at first—it was more a case of engineers and management finding an excuse to 'think aloud'. In every way—literally, in every detail—it was different from any previous Rootes car, and from any of its competitors, and that, in the end, was the major problem.

The Rootes Group had never produced a small car in a quarter of a century, when B. B. Winter encouraged two of his keenest young engineers, Mike Parkes and Tim Fry, to build a low-budget minimal-price prototype. Until 1955 the smallest Rootes cars had always been Minxes, and these had been growing, slowly and inexorably, with every model change. Even so, there was no rush to plug the gap at the bottom of the Rootes range. The family were anxious to expand, but were too heavily committed with new Sunbeams and Humbers to tackle it at once. As Mike Parkes once said in a *Motor* interview published in 1968:

'The Rootes Group still had no intention of making a small car. This was merely a wish on the part of the directors to have something put up to them, so that they would know what sort of car could be made, and roughly what its performance would be.'

At which point his collaborator, Tim Fry, chipped in with:

'Didn't they ask for a car capable of carrying two adults and two children at 60mph and 60mpg?'

Parkes's reply to this was that this requirement had evolved following his first meeting with Geoffrey Rootes to report that an ultra-small car was feasible. Work then went ahead in a workshop at Ryton-on-Dunsmore, several miles away from the main Humber

Road development centre, and by the end of 1956 the first 'Slug' was ready for demonstration to the directors. To get down to a cost below any of the rivals (and this meant pricing a car below the Ford Anglias and Austin A30s of the day), Parkes and Fry had chosen a unit-construction body chassis unit, a rear engine/gearbox layout, with swing axle front suspension and swing axle rear suspension. The engine itself was to be a specially designed air-cooled Villiers flat-twin of 600cc, but to get the show on the road a Citroën 2CV engine of 425cc was purchased and installed where the Villiers would have to go.

At first the directors hated everything about the car—its looks, its handling, its specification and its styling. Even after the Pressed Steel Company had got involved in the engineering of a body, and the Rootes styling department had had a go at the looks of the car, it was still not an attractive proposition. It was not until Mike Parkes obtained a Coventry-Climax FWMA light-alloy single-overhead-camshaft engine (which was a prototype racing sports car engine of a mere 741cc) that the project began to make sense.

By 1960, the project had taken on a momentum of its own. 'B.B.' had retired, Peter Ware had taken his place, the Rootes family had

Story (almost) without words—a Devonshire House display of successful Rootes cars from the Monte Carlo Rally. The Imp was David Pollard's 998 cc Group 3 team car, second in its class to Pat Moss-Carlsson's Saab, while the Tiger was Andrew Cowan's, which took eleventh place; in the same event, incidentally, Peter Harper's identical Tiger finished fourth overall, and was on its way to a TV rallycross event in Sweden

seen the roaring success achieved by BMC with the Mini, and they
had decided to expand mightily into the small-car market. It was
at this point that 'Slug' turned into 'Apex', with an official Rootes
development title, and that productionizing of the design began
under the leadership of Leo Kuzmicki, who had originally made
his name with racing Manx Norton motorcycle engines and the
Vanwall Grand Prix engine design. Wheels went up from 10in to
12in diameter, the Rootes family fell for the styling of the rear-
engined Chevrolet Corvair and demanded a look-alike version for
their tiny saloon; it took on width, wheelbase, a more sophisticated
rear suspension (by semi-trailing arms and coil springs) and the
rights to make a Rootes version of the engine were gained from
Coventry-Climax. At the same time the capacity was pushed up—
to 875cc from 741cc—(the FWMA's cylinder dimensions were
64.3 × 57.2mm bore and stroke, that of the true Imp engine became
68 × 60.35mm) and the engine was considerably de-tuned to bring
the performance back *down* to a reasonable level!

In the meantime, Rootes wanted to build a new factory to make
the production cars. They dearly wished to expand their facilities
at Ryton, but were refused permission by the authorities, and were
forced towards one of several 'development areas' located in areas
of high unemployment. The choice was confined to South Wales,
Merseyside or Clydeside, and after a great deal of bargaining the
Rootes family were persuaded to choose a site at Linwood, near
Paisley, on the south bank of the Clyde, downstream of Glasgow,
in exchange for a large Government loan and other industrial
inducements. The factory itself, and the tooling installed therein,
cost £25.5 million, and it was no coincidence that it was built
alongside an existing Pressed Steel Company factory (already
supplying Rover P5 and Volvo P-1800 bodyshells, as well as building railway wagons and carriages), who could supply complete
shells by overhead conveyor to the Rootes factory. Pre-production
began early in 1963, and the Imp (as the Apex had come to be
named) was officially launched on 2 May, when the factory was
opened by HRH Prince Philip, Duke of Edinburgh.

Although the press received the Imp with much kindness, not
to say unrestricted enthusiasm, it soon became clear that its fine
roadholding and very spirited small-car performance could not
balance its doubtful quality of construction and the appalling
reliability record that it gained almost at once. If it was not a case
of water leaks it was cylinder head gaskets blowing, and if it was
not the pneumatic throttle linkage giving trouble it was the water
pumps giving up the ghost. Worse than this, the Imp did not sell
in anything like the 3000-a-week quantities needed to ensure
profitability, for the British public were not to be convinced that a
rear-engined car could handle and perform in the same way as the
Minis, which they had grown accustomed to in the previous three
years. Rootes, already severely damaged by the long strike at
BLSP in London during 1961, were already at the top of the

One of the many privately-entered Hillman Imps to go rallying in the mid-1960s was this 875cc example in the 1964 Alpine Rally. This car isn't much modified

slippery slope to financial ruin which swept them throughout the 1960s.

In the beginning, however, Rootes not only considered badge-engineering the Imp into several other Singer and Sunbeam versions, but they planned several body derivations as well. All the first Imps were two-door saloons with three-box styling and with the rear engine location very effectively disguised, but in the next few years the saloons were joined by lofty estate cars and delivery vans (using the same basic body pressings) and by a very stylish notchback coupé style which retained the saloon's shape below the Corvair-like waistline. If only the money had been available, and if only the Imp had continued to sell in greater numbers, there might also have been an open two-seater sports car; the 'Asp', as this project was called by the engineers and product planners, looked not unlike the Fiat 850 Spider of the period, and would certainly have made MG's Midget and Triumph's Spitfire look old-fashioned from the day it was released.

Technically, there was little difficulty in developing sporting Imps, for the original Coventry-Climax breathing and valve gear arrangements had well and truly been 'tamed' during development, and reversing the process was straightforward enough. For the autumn of 1966, therefore, Rootes launched the Sunbeam Imp Sport (and the Singer Chamois Sport, which was the same thing with different trim and badges), in which a different camshaft profile, modified cylinder head, twin Zenith-Stromberg carburettors, larger valves and a four-branch exhaust manifold all helped boost the Imp's power from 37bhp (DIN) at 4800rpm to 50bhp (DIN) at 5800rpm. Disc front brakes were never thought necessary on a fast Imp, even though the car's top speed was up to at least 90mph.

In 1967 the Hillman Imp Californian arrived, with standard engine under the sleek notchback coupé body style, but by the end of that year the ultimate quantity-production Imp, the Sunbeam Stiletto, had combined the coupé body style with the 'Sport' engine, along with twin headlamps and a new, unique facia and instrument layout, all for £726, very good value in the only mildly inflationary 1960s. Like the other 'Sports', it also had radial-ply tyres, lowered front suspension, servo-assisted brakes and a great deal of character. My colleague Graham Robson, who worked in Rootes engineering for some time, used one for business transport for years, and even bought it from the factory when he moved on to different activities.

In the meantime, however, all these Imp derivatives had been overshadowed by competition cars, and these are the cars by which the Imp range will most likely be remembered. Norman Garrad's long reign as supremo of the Competitions Department had come to an end in the spring of 1964, when Marcus Chambers joined Rootes from the motor trade. Chambers, let me remind everyone, had been most distinguished and successful manager of the BMC Competitions Department between 1955 and 1961, where the budgets, if not limitless, were certainly more generous than those which existed at Rootes in the 1960s. Chambers's first job was to oversee the Sunbeam Tiger Le Mans project and to develop the Tigers for use in International rallying, but the Rootes family had already realized that the dear old Sunbeam Rapier had been rendered uncompetitive by the lightweight Ford Cortina GTs (and later Lotus-Cortinas) and that it had to be pensioned off. To replace the Rapier, and to keep a Rootes *saloon* car in motor sport, they commanded that the Imp should be developed instead.

It was a tall order. The Imp handled well, but was far too slow in standard form even to win its (1-litre) capacity class, where the BMC Mini-Cooper 970S and similar cars were supreme. Chambers and his department, in conjunction with Leo Kuzmicki's engine designers and development chief Peter Wilson (who had raced team cars for concerns as distinguished as Bristol and BMC in the 1950s), produced a 'rally special' which changed all that. The 'Rallye Imp' of 1965 was the result.

Working on the basis of the standard car, the team produced a rapid and eventually reliable little car which was even more effective on the circuits than it was in rallying. At first in prototype form and (by 1966) as an homologated 'GT' car, the Rallye Imp featured a bored-out 998cc engine which developed 65bhp at 6200rpm, and well before the Imp Sport (1967 model) was put on sale the Rallye Imp also featured lowered front suspension, servo brakes and other details, including the unique feature, never copied on quantity-production cars, of a special instrument panel incorporated in the standard car's facia pressing. Cars to this specification were built in batches in a department cheek-by-jowl with Competitions at the Humber Road factory, and were exported to many

In the 1960s, Imps were raced and rallied with distinction. In this posed shot, a Broadspeed Ford Anglia is between a 'works' rally car (on the right of the picture) and a Fraser Imp racing machine

traditional Rootes markets in addition to being delivered to British customers. Production figures for the Rallye Imp were never revealed (probably because fewer cars were built than were *supposed* to have been built to gain sporting homologation), but were probably in the order of 400–500 units.

Getting the team's rally cars into the winner's circle was almost impossible, as even their own special engines rarely produced more than 75bhp in homologated form, or up to about 90bhp when fitted with exotic twin-choke Weber carburettor equipment and similar goodies. The competition (from 130bhp 1275S Mini-Coopers, 160bhp Lotus-Cortinas and similar European projectiles) was just too fast.

Even so, in 1965, the redoubtable Rosemary Smith took advantage of a favourable handicap, the atrocious weather in the French and Swiss mountains, and a great deal of astute team management, to win the Tulip Rally outright. Miss Smith became something of a specialist with the Rallye Imps, albeit with a great deal of cynicism about her own abilities and that of the car (she habitually carried train and airline timetables in her bag—'just in case'), and gained many class and ladies' prizes in the late 1960s.

Peter Harper, Andrew Cowan and latterly Colin Malkin all achieved great things with Rallye Imps. In particular, in 1968, where the regulations allowed the cars to be considerably modified, Malkin won the prestigious *Motoring News* rally championship outright.

Imp Sports and Stilettos with twin carburettors and oil coolers in this engine bay had little space to spare, and cooling was something of a problem

It was on the race tracks of Britain, however, and in the advantageous environment of TV-sponsored rallycross, that the Rallye Imp made the most headlines. There had been early private attempts to race Imps before Rootes dealer Alan Fraser tackled the job seriously in 1965. For 1966, when the British Saloon Car Championship was also to be graced with the presence of highly tuned Broadspeed Ford Anglias, Fraser was given the task of beating them in an 'official' team effort. In this series, and in other events, Fraser Imps of 998cc driven by Ray Calcutt, Nick Brittan and Bernard Unett, gained 30 wins, 19 second places and 13 third places. Two British 'free-for-all' championships were won outright, and it was only after a titanic struggle that Unett's Fraser Imp lost the British Saloon Car championship class to John Fitzpatrick's Ford Anglia.

It was much the same story in 1967. As before, FIA 'Group 5' rules applied, which meant that virtually anything could be done to modify the power train and the suspension. The result was that Fraser Imps regularly developed 115bhp at 9000rpm from their 998cc engines (and neither of those figures is a misprint), and were so highly tuned that they were extremely reluctant even to run below about 4000rpm. This, matched to a *five*-speed (Jack Knight) gearbox cluster, 7in-diameter front wheel disc brakes, 13in wheel rims and racing tyres, made the incredibly versatile Imp into a real racing car. Top speed, suitably geared, was well over 120mph, and it was only the fact that the competing Anglias could use fuel injection, 124bhp, and limited-slip differentials which ensured a straight fight.

In that year, Unett and Tony Lanfranchi battled throughout the season with the Broadspeed Anglias, and once again the result was in doubt until the end of the year. The Imps won three of the ten encounters, and Unett lost the class by a whisker.

Soon after this, Rootes competition policy changed, the limitations of the Rallye Imp were recognised, and the surpise London–Sydney Marathon success in the Hillman Hunter completed the transformation. For a time, even, the Competitions Department went into suspended animation, and when it reopened in the 1970s the accent was on Avengers. In the meantime, however, there was still time for private engine builders to produce an Imp for Bill McGovern to win the British Saloon Car Championship (on points) on several occasions, and a great young rally driver called Henri Toivonen tackled his first serious events in Imps prepared for his use in Finland.

It was by this time, too, that Rootes finances were in considerable disarray, and their policies changing at dispiriting intervals. To summarize—Chrysler took a 30 per cent stake in Rootes voting stock in June 1964, and converted this to total control in 1967. By 1968 they were planning to bring Rootes and Simca (of France) closer together, and by 1970 the Rootes name was discarded and Chrysler United Kingdom took its place. While all this was going on, Hillman Hunter, Sunbeam Rapier and Humber Sceptre production was moved from Ryton to Linwood, to make way for the new Avenger, and the Imps, sporting or otherwise, had to take their chance in the space that was left.

Quite rapidly, the sporting Imps, which had never made money for the company, were run down. There were no Singers of any sort after 1970, and the last of the svelte Stilettos was built in 1972. Only the Sunbeam Sport (shorn of its 'Imp' middle name) soldiered on, completely neglected, until 1976, when it, and the Sunbeam Rapier, also died off. Since then, not only has the company name changed again—to Talbot—but there are new owners (Chrysler sold out to Peugeot-Citroën in 1978), and the last vestige of sporting Rootes tradition has been extinguished.

The combination of
Rosemary Smith and a
998cc Rallye Imp won many
prizes in the 1960s. This is
the 1967 Alpine Rally

9

Aftermath: Chrysler's vision!

The last remotely sporting Rootes-sired product was the 'new' Rapier, alias 'new' Alpine GT [not to be confused with yet another later Alpine] in the States—born 1967, died 1976. While no means a great car, it was a decent one, and much better than it's made out to be.

Though the Tiger died a rapid death after the Chrysler takeover, the open 'old' Alpine lingered on into 1968. But sales were winding down fast in the face of vigorous opposition from the usual quarters —Triumph with the TR5/TR250, MG with the MGB and its GT derivation. Chrysler thus forsook the sports car market to those competitors, hitching its Rootes wagon to the forlorn Imp, the innocuous Hillman Hunter (also known as the Sunbeam Arrow in the States), followed by the even more innocuous and considerably more disastrous Hillman Avenger (Plymouth Cricket!).

The rationale behind the 'new Rapier of 1967' made limited sense, but here it is: A small but loyal portion of the British market was wedded to the original Rapier concept of a mid-range, sporty, 4 passenger (really 2 + 2) two-door hardtop; a fairly large portion of the American market was interested in close-coupled sporty compacts like the Ford Mustang, Chevrolet Camaro and Plymouth Barracuda. Capitalizing on that loyalty towards the Sunbeam marque, it might be possible to retain a Rapier-like car in the line while not spending very much money on development, so Chrysler laid a fastback coupé body over the Hillman Hunter chassis platform. The styling was definitely more Chrysler than Rootes, and the nearest approximation to the new Rapier was the by-then-superseded Plymouth Barracuda, dubbed 'glassback' by Detroit stylists.

Using the Hunter saloon bodyshell allowed a surfeit of passenger space and cargo capacity. Though the fastback lacked a hatch and the rear seat was fixed, the boot held 14cu ft of luggage and the rear parcel shelf was deep and commodious. The window line retained the old Rapier feature, being pillarless, although the broad, sloping roof required a fairly thick 'C' pillar. Although most everything aft of the pillar was glass, visibility was not as good as it appeared on

Studio scale model of new Rapier body style, not quite to the final shape. This work was carried out in 1964

Almost finalized 1968-model-year Sunbeam Rapier body style, in model form, with lay figures to give scale. The car remained in production until 1976

the American Alpine GT, because of high-back bucket seats required by the latest federal regulations.

On introduction in Britain in 1967, the new Rapier's five-main-bearing 1725cc engine offered 88bhp, but modifications carried out for 1968 brought output to 94bhp on both Rapier and Alpine GT, 1968 being the first year for the later. A second less well trimmed model was offered in both countries, $175 below the Alpine GT in America (which cost $2535). This was the plain Alpine coupé, developing only 73hp at 4900rpm.

In true Rootes fashion, the Rapier/Alpine GT were elaborately equipped. They offered a burled walnut instrument panel and console, full instrumentation, radial-ply tyres, carpeted boot and courtesy lights everywhere. The cheaper Alpine coupé lacked the several instruments and radials, but was nicely finished for the money. Flow-through ventilation, all-vinyl interior trim, door-to-door carpeting and trip odometer were common to all models. A heater/demister was standard, while whitewalls and radio were options. Transmission options were a three-speed automatic and (in England only) overdrive on third and top gears.

But the age of the engine was starting to tell. Though the Rapier/Alpine got through the standing quarter-mile in 19 seconds at about 70mph, and had a 95mph top speed, *Road & Track* noted that 'It idles roughly when warm and becomes boomy when accelerating hard.' In a word, it was 'buzzy'. The magazine praised the excellent disc front/drum rear brakes, which pulled the car down from 80 in competent manner, and the steering, which was

The first of the new series of fastback four seater coupés based on the Hillman Hunter running gear, the Sunbeam Rapier. Starting with the 1725 formula the car was quite attractive and should have been able to make a dent in the Ford Capri market. It didn't

light and precise. 'Radial tyres are standard but they are small, and they protest loudly in hard, low-speed cornering . . . At higher speeds a degree of roll oversteer takes some of the load off the front end, making it possible to tweak out the tail with the steering wheel and then keep it out with the throttle. If driven violently on a rough road the Alpine gets into trouble with its live axle bouncing around, but on decent roads the handling is pleasant and predictable if not particularly entertaining.'

It should be evident that what *R & T* is yawningly describing is a fanciful Hillman Hunter, and this was reflected in the fact that the Rapier/Alpine GT was never knowingly raced, rallied or driven with vigour anywhere in the world. As a sort of luxury Hunter, it was viable with certain old Rapier fans in England who could at least order it with overdrive, and North Americans who wanted an economical import with out-of-the-ordinary looks. But potential is all it ever had; Chrysler never pushed the cars hard in the States, and a total clean-out and absorption of the separate Rootes dealer network meant the car found no welcome in any American showroom. It's too bad, because a very similar Toyota Corolla coupé was selling like five-cent hamburgers, albeit at a lower price. Neither did Chrysler ever think about shovelling the Valiant V8 into this Sunbeam, though it would have easily fitted; it is likely that the result would have been too close a competitor to the Plymouth Barracuda.

Rootes and Chrysler board members at the Paris Show in 1964, soon after the corporate link-up had been announced. Lord Rootes is third from the right in the picture, Sir Reginald Rootes is second from the left, and the Hon. Geoffrey Rootes is on the extreme right

The Alpine version of 1968 (above) had much less interior and exterior trim than the Rapier on which it was based. Unfortunately the car's fortunes did not improve

The Holbay engined Rapier H120 (left) was a much improved car. Numerous minor modifications plus 105 horsepower injected decent performance for the day into the rather heavy bodyshell. The cars were neither cheap nor, somehow, 'quite right' and the hoped for vast sales did not take place. Too little, too late

For 1970 the walnut facia gave way to a more modern dashboard, which grouped the instruments squarely in front of the driver, and faced the passenger with a solid piece of padded vinyl. The under-facia parcel shelf was retained, while a new console ran between the seats, enclosing the gear lever and ashtray. Racing stripes and formed steel 'rally' wheels joined the option list.

An interesting variation of the Rapier, not allowed the Americans, was the 110bhp Holbay-tuned Rapier H120. This potent production Rapier proved that reserves were left in the old 1.7-litre clockwork yet. Two 40DCOE twin-choke Weber carburettors were mounted on a special inlet manifold and there was a four-branch exhaust manifold with large-bore tailpipe. Holbay went through the engine in detail, modifying and polishing the combustion chambers and ports, fitting special high-temperature valves with dual chrome-vanadium springs, a high-performance camshaft, sports distributor, heavy-duty diaphragm clutch and servo-assist for the brakes. Standard equipment included a Laycock de Normanville heavy-duty overdrive, wide-rim wheels with high-speed radials, reclining front seats and racing stripes. Special accessories were: an oil cooler, fog and spot lamps. The 0–60 time was about 11 seconds. Performance over the standard Rapier was up 20 per cent overall, yet tractability and refinement were not affected. 'With more power than the Le Mans Sunbeams of only a few years ago,' Chrysler declared, 'the H120 is a real GT car at a realistic price.'

But it was the last hurrah.

By 1976, these last of the sporting Rootes cars had passed away, never to return. The Ryton line was dominated by the Avenger and Linwood by the Imp and the underwhelming Hillman Hunter, in various badge-engineered and so-called hot shot guises to cover the Singer, Humber and Sunbeam franchise. The only Humber was the Hunter-based Sceptre, which Rootes called 'astonishing'. Not for the same reason, long-time Humber loyalists agreed. Chrysler's pentastar logo dominated sales floors and hoardings as the company proclaimed, 'This is the start of something big,' in the history of the British Industry: the decline and fall of Rootes.

But the story written in the snowy Alpine passes and the sunny byways of Monte Carlo, on the long straights of Le Mans and Sebring, on the corners at Riverside and Daytona, and at countless lesser venues in both the Old and New World would live.

Appendix I

Averaged performance figures

The following figures are based mainly on *Autocar* and *Road & Track* road tests, with occasional tests by other magazines. Where figures differed, they were invariably averaged; thus it is hoped that we have arrived at a highly accurate picture of each model's capabilities.

Sunbeam	Year	0–50	0–60	¼-mile	Top speed	Mpg (Imp)
Ten	1947	23.4	35.2	25	66	30
2-litre	1947	18.8	30.0	24	72	27
80	1949	24.0	36.4	24.5	73	30
90 Mk I	1948	17.6	26.8	22.5	80	25
90 Mk II	1951	15.7	24.3	23	86	23
90 Mk IIa	1953	13.5	20.8	22.2	81	28
Series III (od)	1955	12.5	18.4	21.4	91	24
Alpine I	1954	13.6	19.0	21.4	91	21
Alpine II (od)	1955	13.4	18.5	20.7	100	20
Rapier	1956	14.9	21.7	22.4	85	34
Rapier R67	1957	12.5	19.4	21.5	85	30
Rapier II (od)	1958	13.1	19.3	21.1	89	31
Rapier III	1959	11.7	16.5	20.7	92	99
Rapier IV	1964	12.0	17.0	20.8	92	24
Rapier V	1966	9.8	15.2	19.5	95	23
New Alpine (od)	1959	10.3	14.0	20.1	99	25.5
Alpine II (od)	1960	10.1	14.2	19.6	97	23.5
Alpine III (od)	1963	10.0	14.5	19.9	97	23.5
Alpine III GT (od)	1963	10.5	15.9	21.6	99	20.6
Alpine IV GT (od)	1964	10.2	13.8	19.2	95	23.5
Alpine IV GT (auto)	1964	13.3	18.8	22.5	92	20.9
Alpine V (od)	1966	9.8	13.6	19.1	100	25.5
Harrington GT	1961	9.6	12.7	19.3	99	24.1
Stage 3 (od)	1961	7.8	10.6	17.9	109	22.0
Harrington le Mans	1962	9.7	13.1	19.6	107	19.5
Tiger 260	1964	6.3	8.9	16.0	118	20.0
Tiger 289	1967	5.6	7.5	16.0	122	21.6
New Rapier	1967	9.0	13.5	18.7	103	26.6
Rapier H120	1968	7.8	10.5	17.7	105	21.9
Alpine coupé	1969	10.2	14.3	19.9	91	25.9

Appendix 2
Rootes specifications

Sunbeam-Talbot 10—produced 1945–48 (also produced 1938–39 as body style, and chassis dates from 1935)

Technical description: *The Autocar*, 10.8.45

Engine: 4-cyl, 63 × 95mm, 1185cc, side-valves. CR 6.8:1, Stromberg carb, 41bhp at 4500rpm. Torque not disclosed.
Transmission: Axle ratio 5.22. Overall ratios 5.22, 7.77, 12.9, 18.63, reverse 24.83:1. 14.6mph/1000rpm in top gear.
Suspension and brakes: Beam front axle, half-elliptic leaf springs, lever arm dampers: live rear axle, half-elliptic leaf springs, lever arm dampers. Worm and nut steering. 8in-diameter drum brakes at front and rear. 5.25–16in tyres on 3.5in rims.
Dimensions: Wheelbase 7ft 10in; front track 3ft 10.9in; rear track 4ft 0.5in. Length 13ft 0in; width 5ft 0in; height 4ft 10.5in. Unladen weight 2185lb.
Performance: (*The Autocar*, 7.2.47) Maximum speed 66mph. 0–60mph 35.2sec. Standing ¼-mile 25sec. Fuel consumption about 30mpg.
Price: Saloon £684 in 1946
      DHC £729 in 1946 (Prices *include* Purchase
      Tourer £646 in 1946 Tax)

Sunbeam-Talbot 2-litre—produced 1945–48 (also produced very briefly, 1939)

Engine: 4-cyl, 75 × 110mm, 1944cc, side-valves, CR 6.4:1, Stromberg carb, 56bhp at 3800rpm. Torque not disclosed.
Transmission: Axle ratio 4.44. Overall ratios 4.44, 6.62, 10.97, 15.83, reverse 21.12:1. 17.2mph 1000rpm in top gear.
Suspension and brakes: Beam front axle, hall-elliptic leaf springs, lever arm dampers; live rear axle, half-elliptic leaf springs, lever arm dampers. Worm and nut steering. 10in-diameter drum brakes at front and rear. 5.25–16in tyres on 3.5in rims.

Dimensions: Wheelbase 8ft 1.5in; front track 3ft 10.9in; rear track 4ft 0.5in. Length 13ft 2.5in; width 5ft 0in; height 4ft 10.5in. Unladen weight 2490lb.
Performance: (*The Autocar*, 17.1.47) Maximum speed 72mph. 0–60mph approx 30sec. Standing ¼-mile approx 24sec. Fuel consumption about 27mpg.
Price: Saloon £799 in 1946
      DHC £844 in 1946
      Tourer £761 in 1946

(Note: 10 and 2-litre shared same chassis and body styles, except that 2-litre had longer wheelbase/longer nose to accommodate the larger 1944cc engine. Passenger cabin was the same for each type.)

Sunbeam-Talbot 80—produced 1948–50

Technical description: *The Autocar*, 2.7.48.

Engine: 4-cyl, 63 × 95mm, 1185cc, overhead valves. CR 6.9:1, Solex carb, 47bhp at 4800rpm. Torque not disclosed.
Transmission: Axle ratio 5.22. Overall ratios 5.22, 7.77, 12.9, 18.63, reverse 24.83:1. 14.9mph/1000rpm in top gear.
Suspension: Beam front axle, half-elliptic leaf springs, lever arm dampers; live rear axle, half-elliptic leaf springs, lever arm dampers. Worm and nut steering. 9in-diameter drum brakes at front and rear. 5.50–16in tyres on 4.0in rims.
Dimensions: Wheelbase 8ft 1.5in; front track 3ft 11.5in; rear track 4ft 2.5in. Length 13ft 11.5in; width 5ft 2.5in; height 5ft 0.75in. Unladen weight 2605lb.
Performance: (*The Autocar*, 18.2.49) Maximum speed 73mph. 0–60mph 36.4sec. Standing ¼-mile 24.5sec. Fuel consumption about 30mpg.
Price: Saloon £889 in 1948
      DHC £953 in 1958

Sunbeam-Talbot 90 Mk I—produced 1948–50

Engine: 4-cyl, 75 × 110mm, 1944cc, overhead valves, CR 6.6:1, Stromberg carb, 64bhp at 4100rpm. Torque not disclosed.
Transmission: Axle ratio 4.3. Overall ratios 4.3, 6.41, 10.62, 15.32, reverse 20.45:1. 18.05mph/1000rpm in top gear.
Suspension and brakes: Beam front axle, half-elliptic leaf springs, lever arm dampers; live rear axle, half-elliptic leaf springs, lever arm dampers. Worm and nut steering. 10in-diameter drum brakes at front and rear. 5.50–16in tyres on 4.0in rims.
Dimensions: Wheelbase 8ft 1.5in; front track 3ft 11.5in; rear track 4ft 2.5in. Length 13ft 11.5in; width 5 ft 2.5in; height 5ft 0.75in. Unladen weight 2830lb.
Performance: (*The Autocar*, 2.7.48) Maximum speed 80mph. 0–60mph 26.8sec. Standing ¼-mile 22.5sec. Fuel consumption about 25mpg.
Price: Saloon   £991 in 1948
       DHC   £1054 in 1948

(Note: 80 and 90 Mk I were effectively the same cars except for the engines, that of the 80 being an ohv version of the Minx, that of the 90 being an ohv version of the Humber Hawk. Everything else—chassis, suspensions, bodies, gearbox and axle casing—was the same.)

Sunbeam-Talbot 90 Mk II—produced 1950–52

Technical description: *The Autocar*, 22.9.50

Engine: 4-cyl, 81 × 110mm, 2267cc, overhead valves, CR 6.5:1, Stromberg carb, 70bhp at 4000rpm, 113lb ft torque at 2400rpm.
Transmission: Axle ratio 3.9. Overall ratios 3.9, 5.81, 9.633, 13.9, reverse 18.55:1. 19.9mph/1000rpm in top gear.
Suspension and brakes: Ifs, coil springs, wishbones, anti-roll bar; live rear axle, half-elliptic leaf springs, Panhard rod, lever arm dampers. Recirculating ball steering. 10in-diameter drum brakes at front and rear. 5.50–16in tyres on 4.0in rims.
Dimensions: Wheelbase 8ft 1.5in; front track 3ft 11.5in; rear track 4ft 2.5in. Length 13ft 11.5in; width 5ft 2.5in; height 5ft 0.75in. Unladen weight 2905lb.
Performance: (*The Autocar*, 21.2.51) Maximum speed 86mph. 0–60mph 24.3sec. Standing ¼-mile 23sec. Fuel consumption about 23mpg.
Price: Saloon   £991 in 1950
       DHC   £1054 in 1950

(Note: No style changes from Mk I, but new chassis frame with independent suspension underneath, new hypoid bevel axle—previous S-Ts had spiral bevel axles—and enlarged Hawk-type engine.)

(Note: S-T 80 was not continued after 1950.)

Sunbeam-Talbot 90 Mk IIA—produced 1952–54

CR 7.7:1, 77bhp at 4100rpm. Changes from Mk II were: Deletion of rear wheel spats or skirts, perforated road wheels, and use of brakes with 2¼in-wide linings instead of 1¾in-wide linings.
Performance: (*The Autocar*, 6.3.53) Maximum speed 81mph. 0–60mph 20.8sec. Standing ¼-mile 22.2sec. Fuel consumption about 28mpg.
Price: Saloon   £1347 in 1952
       DHC   £1394 in 1952

Sunbeam Mk III—produced 1954–57
(*The Autocar*: 8.10.54)

Changes from Mk IIA were: CR 7.5:1. 80bhp at 4400rpm. Maximum torque 122lb ft at 2400rpm. Stromberg carb. Overall ratios 3.9, 5.81, 9.63, 12.43, reverse 12.43:1. Optional Laycock overdrive, with 4.22 axle. Overall ratios 3.28, 4.22, 6.30, 10.43, 13.45, reverse 17.04:1. 23.8mph/1000rpm in overdrive top gear. Tyres fitted to 4.5in rims. Unladen weight 2950lb.
Performance: (Overdrive model, *The Autocar*: 11.3.55) Maximum speed 91mph. 0–60mph 18.4sec. Standing ¼-mile 21.4sec. Fuel consumption about 24mpg.
Price: Saloon   £1127 in 1954   (Overdrive £64 extra)
       DHC   £1198 in 1954

(Note: Sunbeam Mk III was same car as Sunbeam-Talbot Mk IIA except for changes listed above.)

Sunbeam Alpine 2-seater sports—produced 1953–55

Technical description: *The Autocar*, 20.3.53

Basic chassis and style specification as for S-T 90 Mk IIA, except for: CR 7.4:1, 80bhp at 4200rpm, maximum torque 124lb ft at 1800rpm. Overall gear ratios 3.9, 5.19, 8.54, 11.04, reverse 13.96:1. 20.1mph/1000rpm in top gear. 4.5in wheel rims. Height 4ft 8in. Unladen weight 2900lb.
Performance: (*The Autocar*, 23.4.54) Maximum speed 95mph. 0–60mph 18.9sec. Standing ¼-mile 21.1sec. Fuel consumption about 24mpg.
Price: 2-seater £1269 in 1954.

(Note: Overdrive became standard from autumn 1954. Overall ratios 3.28, 4.22, 5.62, 9.24, 11.95, reverse 15.11:1. 23.90mph/1000rpm in overdrive top gear.)

Sunbeam Rapier I—produced 1955–57

Technical description: *The Autocar*, 14.10.55

Engine: 4-cyl, 76.2 × 76.2mm, 1390cc, overhead valves, CR 8.0:1, Stromberg carburettor, 62.5bhp (gross), 57.5bhp (net) at 5000rpm. Maximum torque 73lb ft at 3000rpm.
Transmission: Axle ratio 5.22. Overall ratios, including overdrive, 3.95, 5.22, (o/d 3rd) 5.89, 7.78, 16.64, reverse 21.08:1. 14.0mph/1000rpm in direct top gear, 18.52 in o/d top.
Suspension and brakes: Ifs, coil springs, wishbones, anti-roll bar and telescopic dampers; live rear axle, half-elliptic leaf springs, and telescopic dampers. Worm and nut steering. 9in diameter and 1.75in-width drum brakes at front and rear. 5.60–15in tyres on 4.0in rims.
Dimensions: Wheelbase 8ft 0in; front track 4ft 1in; rear track 4ft 0.5in. Length 13ft 4.5in; width 5ft 0.75in; height 4ft 10in. Unladen weight 2280lb.
Performance: (*The Autocar*, 20.4.56) Maximum speed 85mph. 0–60mph 21.7sec. Standing ¼-mile 22.4sec. Fuel consumption about 34mpg.
Price: 2-door coupé £1044 in 1955

(Note: From autumn 1956, the following changes were introduced: two Zenith carbs, 67bhp (gross) at 5400rpm; maximum torque 74lb ft at 3000rpm.)

Performance: (*The Autocar*, 1.2.57) Maximum speed 85mph. 0–60mph 19.4sec. Standing ¼-mile 21.5sec. Fuel consumption about 30mpg.

Sunbeam Rapier II—produced 1958–59

Technical description: *The Autocar*, 7.2.58

Engine: 4-cyl, 79 × 76.2mm, 1494cc, overhead valves, CR 8.5:1, two Zenith carbs, 73bhp (gross), 68bhp (net) at 5200rpm; maximum torque 81 at 3000rpm.
Transmission: Axle ratio 4.78. Overall ratios, including overdrive, 3.61, 4.78, (o/d 3rd) 5.387, 7.126, 11.807, 15.227, reverse 19.288:1. If overdrive not fitted, axle ratio 4.55. Overall ratios, 4.55, 6.794, 11.258, 14.518, reverse 18.389:1. 16.1mph/1000rpm in direct top gear. 20.3mph/1000rpm in overdrive top gear.
Suspension and brakes: Ifs, coil springs, wishbones, anti-roll bar and telescopic dampers; live rear axle, half-elliptic leaf springs, telescopic dampers. Recirculating ball steering. 10 × 2¼in front drum brakes, 9 × 1¾in rear drum brakes. 5.60–15in tyres on 4.0in rims.
Dimensions: Wheelbase 8ft 0in; front track 4ft 1in; rear track 4ft 0.5in. Length 13ft 6.5in; width 5ft 0.75in; height 4ft 10in. Unladen weight 2280lb (coupé), 2275lb (convertible).

Performance: (*The Autocar*, 28.3.58) Maximum speed 90mph. 0–60mph 20.2sec. Standing ¼-mile 21.1sec. Fuel consumption about 32mpg.
Price: Coupé £1044 in 1958
DHC £1104 in 1958

Sunbeam Rapier III—produced 1959–61

Technical description: *The Autocar*, 11.9.59

Specification as for Rapier II, except for: CR9.2:1, 78bhp (gross), 73bhp (net) at 5400rpm; maximum torque 83lb ft at 3500rpm.
Transmission: With or without overdrive. Without overdrive, axle ratio 4.55, overall ratios 4.55, 6.34, 9.75, 15.24, reverse 19.30:1. With overdrive, axle ratio 4.78, overall ratios 3.84, 4.78, (o/d 3rd) 5.33, 6.65, 10.22, 15.98, reverse 20.25:1. 16.1mph/1000rpm in top gear without overdrive. 19.1mph/1000rpm in overdrive top gear if overdrive fitted.
Brakes: 10.8in diameter front discs, 9 × 11¾in rear drums.
Dimensions: Front track 4ft 1.75in. Unladen weight (coupé) 2340lb (convertible) 2362lb.
Performance: (*The Autocar*, 27.11.59) Maximum speed 92mph. 0–60mph 16.5sec. Standing ¼-mile 20.7sec. Fuel consumption about 29mpg.
Price: Coupé £986 in 1959
DHC £1042 in 1959

Sunbeam Rapier IIIA—produced 1961–63

Technical description: *The Autocar*, 21.4.61

Specifications as for Rapier III, except for the following engine changes:
81.5 × 76.2mm, 1592cc. CR 9.1:1. 80bhp (gross), 75bhp (net) at 5,100 rpm; maximum torque 88lb ft at 3900rpm.
Price: Coupé £1000 in 1961
DHC £1057 in 1961

Sunbeam Rapier IV—produced 1963–65

Technical description: *The Autocar*, 18.10.63

Basic specification as for Series III and IIIA Rapiers, but complete specification as follows:
Engine: 4-cyl, 81.5 × 76.2mm, 1592cc, overhead valves, CR 9.1:1, Solex compound carb, 78.5bhp (net) at 5000rpm; maximum torque 91lb ft at 3500rpm.
Transmission: With or without overdrive. Without overdrive, axle ratio 3.89. Overall ratios 3.89, 5.41, 8.32, 13.01, reverse 16.48:1. With overdrive, axle ratio 4.22, overall ratios 3.39, 4.22, (o/d 3rd) 4.72, 5.88, 9.04, 14.13, reverse 17.90:1. 17.6mph/1000rpm

Typical Rootes Group advertisement of the period. Their competition successes were important to them

in non-overdrive direct top gear. 20.2mph/1000rpm in overdrive top gear.

Suspension and brakes: Ifs, coil springs, wishbones, anti-roll bar and telescopic dampers; live rear axle, half-elliptic leaf springs, telescopic dampers. Recirculating ball steering. 10.3in front disc brakes, $9 \times 1\frac{3}{4}$in rear drums. 6.00-13in wheels on 4.5in rims. Dimensions: Wheelbase 8ft 0in; front track 4ft 3.75in; rear track 4ft 0.5in. Length 13ft 7.25in; width 5ft

0.75in; height 4ft 9.25in. Unladen weight 2300lb. (Note: No convertible version available.)

Performance: (*The Autocar*, 24.7.64) Maximum speed 92mph. 0–60mph 17.0sec. Standing $\frac{1}{4}$-mile 20.8sec. Fuel consumption about 24mpg.

Price: Coupé £877 in 1963

(Note: From autumn 1964, an all-synchromesh gearbox was fitted. There were no ratio changes.)

Sunbeam Rapier V—produced 1965–67

Technical description: *The Autocar*, 10.9.65

Specification as for Rapier IV, except for:
81.5 × 82.55mm, 1725cc. CR 9.2:1. 85bhp (net) at
5500rpm; maximum torque 99lb ft at 3500rpm.
Engine had five main bearings, in place of three main
bearings of all other earlier Rapier engines.

(Note: All Rapiers Series I to V, built between 1955
and 1967, were based on the same chassis, body and
styling layouts. Changes from series to series were
gradual, and the links were obvious.

All such Rapiers were two-door models, derived
from the four-door Hillman Minx models.

The Sunbeam Alpine two-seaters of 1959–68,
descriptions of which follow below, were effectively
based on a short-wheelbase derivative of the same
'chassis'.)

Sunbeam Alpine I—produced 1959–60

Technical description: *The Autocar*, 21.8.59

Engine:4-cyl, 79 × 76.2mm, 1494cc, overhead valves,
CR 9.2:1, two Zenith carbs, 83.5bhp (gross), 78bhp
(net) at 5300rpm; maximum torque 89lb ft at
3400rpm.
Transmission: With or without overdrive. Without
overdrive, axle ratio 3.90. Overall ratios 3.90, 5.41,
8.32, 13.01, reverse 16.48:1. With overdrive, axle
ratio 4.22. Overall ratios 3.38, 4.22, (o/d 3rd), 4.72,
5.88, 9.04, 14.13, reverse 17.90:1. 17.2mph/1000rpm
in non-overdrive top gear. 19.9mph/1000rpm in
overdrive top gear.
Suspension and brakes: Ifs, coil springs, wishbones,
anti-roll bar, telescopic dampers; live rear axle, half-
elliptic leaf springs, telescopic dampers. Recirculating
ball steering. 9.5in front disc brakes, 9 × 1¾in rear
drum brakes. 5.60–13in tyres on 4.5in rims.
Dimensions: Wheelbase 7ft 2in; front track 4ft 3in;
rear track 4ft 0.5in. Length 12ft 11.25in; width
5ft 0.5in; height 4ft 3.5in. Unladen weight 2135lb.
Performance: (*The Autocar*, 4.9.59) Maximum speed
98mph. 0–60mph 14.0sec. Standing ¼-mile 19.8sec.
Fuel consumption about 26mpg.
Price: Sports car £972 in 1959

Sunbeam Alpine II—produced 1960–63

Technical description: *The Autocar*, 21.10.60

Basic specification as for Alpine I except for:
81.5 × 76.2mm, 1592cc, CR 9.1:1, 85.5bhp (gross),
80bhp (net) at 5000rpm; maximum torque 94lb ft at
3800rpm.
Performance: (*The Autocar*, 2.12.60) Maximum speed
97mph. 0–60mph 14.8sec. Standing ¼-mile 19.7sec.
Fuel consumption about 22mpg.
Price: Sports car £986 in 1960

Sunbeam Alpine III—produced 1963–64

Technical description: *The Autocar*, 15.3.63

Basic specification as for Alpine II except for:
Open sports: 87.8bhp (gross) at 5000rpm; maximum
torque 94lb ft at 3800rpm.
GT Coupé: 80.3bhp (gross) at 5000rpm; maximum
torque 91lb ft at 3500rpm.
Transmission with or without overdrive. Axle ratio in
each case 3.89:1. Overall ratios (overdrive top) 3.12,
3.89, (o/d 3rd) 3.85, 4.80, 7.38, 11.35, reverse 14.61:1.
17.6mph/1000rpm in direct top gear, 21.9mph/
1000rpm in overdrive top gear. 5.90–13in tyres or
6.00–13in wheels. Unladen weight (Sports) 2155lb,
(GT) 2240lb.
Performance: (GT version, *The Autocar*, 20.9.63)
Maximum speed 98mph. 0–60mph 14.9sec. Standing
¼-mile 19.8sec. Fuel consumption about 25mpg.
Price: Sports car £840 in 1963
GT Coupé £900 in 1963

Sunbeam Alpine IV—produced 1964–65

Technical description: *The Autocar*, 17.1.64

Basic specification as for Alpine III except for:
Engine: (both versions) 87.5bhp (gross) at 5000rpm;
maximum torque 93lb ft at 3500rpm. One Solex
compound carburettor.
Transmission: With and without overdrive, or with
optional Borg Warner automatic box. Axle ratio: 3.89
without overdrive, and with automatic, 4.22 with
overdrive. Overall ratios, without overdrive: 3.89,
5.41, 8.32, 13.01;1, reverse 16.48:1. With overdrive:
3.39, 4.22, (o/d 3rd) 4.72, 5.88, 9.04, 14.13, reverse
17.90:1. With automatic 3.89, 5.64, 9.31, reverse
8.14:1. 17.6mph/1000rpm in non-overdrive top gear,
or with automatic transmission. 20.2mph/1000rpm in
overdrive top gear.
Performance: (Automatic version, *The Autocar*,
22.5.64) Maximum speed 92mph. 0–60mph 18.8sec.
Standing ¼-mile 22.5sec. Fuel consumption about
22mpg.
Price: Sports car £852 in 1964
GT Coupé £913 in 1964

(Note: From autumn 1964 an all-synchromesh
manual gearbox was fitted. There were no changes in
overall ratios.)

Sunbeam Alpine V—produced 1965–68

Technical description: *The Autocar*, 10.9.65

Basic specification as for Alpine IV, except for:
81.5 × 82.55mm, 1725cc, CR 9.2:1. Maximum power
92.5bhp (net) at 5500rpm; maximum torque 103lb ft
at 3700rpm. Twin Stromberg constant-vacuum
carburettors.

Transmission: With and without overdrive, but *no* automatic transmission. Axle ratio without overdrive 3.89. Overall ratios 3.89, 5.04, 7.75, 12.14, reverse 13.03:1. Axle ratio with overdrive 4.22. Overall ratios 3.39, 4.22, (o/d 3rd) 4.39, 5.47, 8.40, 13.17, reverse 14.14:1.
Performance: (*The Autocar*, 13.5.66) Maximum speed 98mph. 0–60mph 13.6sec. Standing $\frac{1}{4}$-mile 19.1sec. Fuel consumption about 26mpg.
Price: Sports   £878 in 1965
          GT Coupé £938 in 1965

(Note: All Alpines Series I to V, built between 1959 and 1968, were based on the same 'chassis', body and styling layout. Changes from series to series were gradual, and the links were obvious. The engine, in particular, gradually evolved from 1494cc to 1725cc.

All Alpines were two-door two-seaters. Most were open sports cars, but the Series III/IV/V GTs had metal hardtops which could nevertheless be detached.

Note: The engine was basically a three-bearing unit, but was converted to five-bearing when the stretch to 1725cc was made.

Although gear ratios look illogical, they are all, indeed, correct. In particular, the Series III is something of an anomaly, with no special 'overdrive' axle ratio, and with the temporary use of close ratio gears.)

Sunbeam Tiger I—produced 1964–66

Technical description: *The Autocar*, 10.4.64

Car based on bodyshell of Sunbeam Alpine SIV of 1964. Full specification, however, was:
Engine: V8-cyl, by Ford of USA, 96.5 × 73mm, 4261cc, overhead valves, CR 8.8:1, Ford carburettor, 164bhp (gross) at 4400rpm; maximum torque 258lb ft at 2200rpm.
Transmission: Axle ratio 2.88:1. Overall ratios 2.88, 3.72, 4.87, 6.68, reverse 6.68:1. 23.2mph/1000rpm in top gear.
Suspension and brakes: Ifs, coil springs, wishbones, anti-roll bar, telescopic dampers; live rear axle, half-elliptic leaf springs, Panhard rod, telescopic dampers. Rack-and-pinion steering. 9.85in front disc brakes, 9 × 1.75in rear drum brakes. 5.90–13in tyres on 4.5in wheel rims.
Dimensions: Wheelbase 7ft 2in; front track 4ft 3.75in; rear track 4ft 0.5in. Overall length 13ft 2in (that included overriders), width 5ft 0.5in; height 4ft 3.5in. Unladen weight (Tourer) 2525lb, (GT coupé) 2575lb.
Performance: (*The Autocar*, 30.4.65) Maximum speed 117mph. 0–60mph 9.5sec. Standing $\frac{1}{4}$-mile 17.0sec. Fuel consumption about 17mpg.
Price: Export-only at first
          Open tourer £1446 in 1965
          GT Coupé £1506 in 1965 (Tourer + hardtop)

Sunbeam Tiger II—produced 1966–67

Technical description: *The Autocar*, 9.3.67

Specification as for Tiger I, except for:
101.66 × 73mm, 4727cc, CR 9.3:1, 200bhp (gross) at 4400rpm; 282lb ft torque at 2400rpm. Overall gear ratios 2.88, 3.92, 5.56, 8.00, reverse 8.11:1.
Performance: No British test published, because the car was not sold in GB. Tested in *R&T*, September 1967. RML to research figs.

Sunbeam Rapier (Hunter-based)— produced 1967–76

Technical description: *The Autocar*, 12.10.67

Car based on underframe and suspensions, and general mechanical layout, of Hillman Hunter, launched in autumn 1966.

Engine: 4-cyl, 81.5 × 82.55, 1725cc, overhead valves, CR 9.2:1, 2 Stromberg 150CD carburettors, 88bhp (net) at 5200rpm; maximum torque 100lb ft at 4000rpm.
Transmission: With overdrive as standard. Axle ratio 4.22:1. Overall ratios 3.39, 4.22, (o/d 3rd) 4.38, 5.46, 8.40, 13.16:1. 19.4mph/1000rpm in overdrive top gear. Optional Borg Warner automatic transmission, axle ratio 3.7:1. Overall ratios 3.7, 5.36, 8.84, reverse 7.73:1. 17.0mph/1000rpm in top gear.
Suspension and brakes: Ifs, coil springs, MacPherson struts and anti-roll bar, telescopic dampers; live rear axle, half-elliptic leaf springs, telescopic dampers. Recirculating ball steering. 9.6in front disc brakes, 9 × 1.75in rear drum brakes. 155–13in tyres on 4.5in wheel rims.
Dimensions: Wheelbase 8ft 2.5in; front track 4ft 4in; rear track 4ft 4in. Overall length 14ft 6.5in; width 5ft 4.75in; height 4ft 7in. Unladen weight 2275lb.
Performance: (*The Autocar*, 25.1.68) Maximum speed 103mph. 0–60mph 12.8sec. Standing $\frac{1}{4}$-mile 18.7sec. Fuel consumption about 28mpg.
Price: Coupé £1200 in 1967

From spring 1972, engine changes resulted in: 76bhp (DIN) at 5100rpm; 93lb ft at 3300rpm. DIN rating is more severe than the old (net) rating.

Sunbeam Rapier H120—produced 1968–76

Technical description: *The Autocar*, 17.10.68

Specification basically as for Hunter-based Rapier, except for:
CR 9.6:1, 2 Weber 40DCOE carburettors, 105bhp (net) at 5200rpm; maximum torque 120lb ft at 4000rpm. Axle ratio 3.89:1. Overdrive transmission standard. Overall ratios 3.12, 3.89, (o/d 3rd) 4.04,

5.04, 7.75, 12.14, reverse 12.57:1. Automatic transmission not available. 21.5mph/1000rpm in overdrive top gear.
165–13in tyres on 5in wheel rims.
Unladen weight 2300lb.
Performance: (*The Autocar*, 9.1.69) Maximum speed 105mph. 0–60mph 11.1sec. Standing ¼-mile 17.7sec. Fuel consumption about 24mpg.
Price: Coupé £1644 in 1969

The power output was later recalibrated to DIN standards:
93bhp (DIN) at 5200rpm; maximum torque 106lb ft at 4000rpm.

Sunbeam Alpine (Hunter-based)—produced 1969–76

Technical description: *The Autocar*, 16.10.69

Specification basically as for Hunter-based Rapier, except for:
CR 9.2:1, one Stromberg 150CD carburettor, 74bhp (net) at 5000rpm; maximum torque 96lb ft at 3000rpm. With or without overdrive. Without overdrive, axle ratio 3.89:1. Overall ratios 3.89, 5.41, 8.33, 13.04, reverse 13.88:1. With overdrive, axle ratio and overall ratios as Rapier. Automatic transmission, axle ratio 3.89. Overall ratios 3.89, 5.64, 9.33, reverse 8.13:1. 17.8mph/1000rpm in top gear, 20.6mph/1000rpm in overdrive top gear, 17.8mph/1000rpm in automatic. 6.00–13in tyres. Unladen weight 2220lb.
Performance: (*The Autocar*, 6.11.69) Maximum speed 91mph. 0–60mph 14.6sec. Standing ¼-mile 19.9sec. Fuel consumption about 28mpg.
Price: Coupé £1086 in 1969
Imported to USA, 1969–70 only.
From spring 1972 the engine was (a) tuned up, and (b) recalibrated to DIN standards:
72bhp (DIN) at 5000rpm; maximum torque 90lb ft at 3000rpm. 155–13in tyres became standard.

Hillman GT—produced 1969–70

Technical description: *The Autocar*, 2.10.69

Specification based on the basic Hillman Hunter.
Full specification:
Engine: 4-cyl, 81.5 × 82.55mm, 1725cc, overhead valves, CR 9.2:1, 2 Stromberg 150CD carburettors, 88bhp (net) at 5200rpm; maximum torque 100lb ft at 4000rpm.
Transmission: With or without overdrive. Without overdrive, axle ratio 3.7:1. Overall ratios 3.7, 5.15, 7.93, 12.41, 13.2:1. With overdrive, axle ratio 3.89:1. Overall ratios 3.12, 3.89, (o/d 3rd) 4.35, 5.41, 8.33, 12.07, reverse 13.89:1. 18.2mph/1000rpm in direct top gear. 21.6mph/1000rpm in overdrive top gear.

Suspension and brakes: Ifs, coil springs, MacPherson struts and anti-roll bar, telescopic dampers; live rear axle, half-elliptic leaf springs, telescopic dampers. Recirculating ball steering. 9.6in front disc brakes, 9 × 1.75in rear drum brakes. 165–13in tyres on 4.5in rims.
Dimensions: Wheelbase 8ft 2.5in; front track 4ft 4in; rear track 4ft 4in. Overall length 14ft 0in; width 5ft 3.5in; height 4ft 8in. Unladen weight 2100lb.
Performance: (*The Autocar*, 2.10.69) Maximum speed 96mph. 0–60mph 13.9sec. Standing ¼-mile 19.4sec. Fuel consumption about 24mpg.
Price: Saloon £970 in 1969

(Note: From autumn 1970 (i.e. for 1971 model year) the car was renamed Hillman Hunter GT. Produced: 1970–75.)

(Note: From spring 1972, rationalization and recalibration resulted in engine power being quoted as 79bhp (DIN) at 5100rpm; maximum torque 93lb ft at 3300rpm.)

Hillman Hunter GLS—produced 1972–76

Basic specification as for Hunter GT, except for:
H120 engine, two Weber carbs, CR 9.6:1, 93bhp (DIN) at 5200rpm; maximum torque 106lb ft at 4000rpm. With or without overdrive. Without overdrive, axle ratio 3.7:1. Overall ratios 3.7, 4.79, 7.38, 11.56, reverse 12.30:1. With overdrive, axle ratio 3.89:1. Overall ratios 3.12, 3.89, (o/d 3rd) 4.04, 5.04, 7.75, 12.14, reverse 12.57:1. (Note: Hunter GT also made with these ratios from spring 1972.) 165–13in on 5.0in wheel rims. Unladen weight 2090lb.
Performance: (*The Autocar*, 11.5.72) Maximum speed 108mph. 0–60mph 10.5sec. Standing ¼-mile 17.4sec. Fuel consumption about 24mpg.
Price: Saloon £1293 in 1972

Sunbeam Imp Sport/Sunbeam Sport/Singer Chamois Sport—produced 1966–76

Technical description. (Imp, *The Autocar*, 3.5.63, Imp Sport, *The Autocar*, 7.10.66)

Specification based on that of basic Hillman Imp. Three different models marketed, all mechanically identical, but with different 'badge engineering' details.

Full specification:
Engine: 4-cyl, 68 × 60.4mm, 875cc, single overhead camshaft valve operation, CR 10.0:1, 2 Stromberg 125CD carburettors, 51bhp (net) at 6100rpm; maximum torque 52lb ft at 4300rpm.
Transmission: Rear engine, rear drive, transmission in unit with engine and final drive. Final drive ratio

4.86:1. Overall ratios 4.14, 5.70, 8.90, 16.59, reverse 13.83:1. 15.1mph/1000rpm in top gear.
Suspension and brakes: Ifs, coil springs, swing axles, telescopic dampers; irs, coil springs, semi-trailing arms, telescopic dampers. Rack-and-pinion steering. 8 × 1.5in drum brakes at front and rear. 155–12in tyres on 4.5in rims.
Dimensions: Wheelbase 6ft 10in; front track 4ft 2.5in; rear track 4ft 0in. Overall length 11ft 7in; width 5ft 0.25in; height 4ft 6.5in. Unladen weight 1655lb.
Performance: (*The Autocar*, 21.10.66) Maximum speed 90mph. 0–60mph 16.3 sec. Standing $\frac{1}{4}$-mile 20.2sec. Fuel consumption about 34mpg.
Price: Sunbeam Imp Sport saloon £665 in 1966

Sunbeam Stiletto—produced 1967–72

Technical description: *The Autocar*, 5.10.67

Specification as for Imp Sport saloon, except for use of restyled coupé top. Overall height 4ft 4.25in. Unladen weight 1625lb.
Performance: (*The Autocar*, 14.12.67) Maximum speed 87mph. 0–60mph 17.6sec. Standing $\frac{1}{4}$-mile 20.5sec. Fuel consumption about 34mpg.
Price: Sports coupé £734 in 1967

Hillman/Sunbeam Rallye Imp—produced 1965–69

No technical description was ever published. This was an 'homologation special', which is to say that it was specially developed for racing and rallying. Several hundred cars were produced by the conversion of standard Imps or Imp Sports, and a department was set up alongside the Comps. Department at the Humber Road factory to achieve this.

Specification as for Imp Sport saloon, except for: 72.5 × 60.4mm, 998cc, 2 Stromberg 150CD carburettors. 60bhp (DIN) at 6200rpm; maximum torque 59lb ft at 3200rpm.
Performance: (Works rally car, virtually 'as standard', *The Autocar*, 28.1.66) Maximum speed 92mph. 0–60mph 14.9sec. Standing $\frac{1}{4}$-mile 19.8sec. Fuel consumption about 30mpg.
Price: There was a conversion extra price over the standard car.

Appendix 3
Humber specifications

Humber Hawk produced 1945–47 (pre-war body style and engineering—style first seen in 1937)

Technical description: *The Autocar*, 3.8.45

Engine: 4-cyl, 75 × 110mm, 1944cc, side valves, CR 6.4:1, Stromberg carb, 56bhp at 3800rpm. Maximum torque 97lb ft at 2000rpm.
Transmission: Axle ratio 4.78:1. Overall ratios 4.78, 7.12, 11.81, 17.02, reverse 22.75:1. 16.4mph/1000rpm in top gear.
Suspension and brakes: Ifs, transverse leaf spring, wishbone upper link, lever arm dampers; live rear axle, half-elliptic leaf springs, anti-roll bar, lever arm dampers. Worm and nut steering. 10in-diameter drum brakes front and rear. 5.75–16in tyres.
Dimensions: Wheelbase 9ft 6in; front track 4ft 7.8in; rear track 4ft 8in. Length 14ft 10in; width 5ft 9in; height 5ft 3in. Unladen weight 2970lb.
Performance: Not tested in this guise.
Price: £684 in 1945 (Note: All prices *include* Purchase Tax)

Humber Hawk Mk II—produced 1947–48

Technical description: *The Autocar*, 26.9.47

Specification as for Mk II, except for new gearbox, also with synchromesh on top, third and second as before, and with same ratios.
Overall length now quoted as 15ft 0in, and height as 5ft 5in, but with no apparent styling changes.
Performance: (*The Autocar*, 26.9.47)
Price: £889 in 1947

Humber Snipe—produced 1945–48

Technical description: *The Autocar*, 3.8.45

Same chassis, suspension, and bodyshell as for 1945–48 Hawk, except for:
Engine: 6-cyl, 69.5 × 120mm, 2731cc, side valves.

CR 6.4:1, Stromberg carb, 65bhp at 3500rpm. Maximum torque 120lb ft at 1300rpm.
Transmission: Axle ratio 4.67:1. Overall ratios 4.67, 6.82, 11.58, 18.35, reverse 18.35:1. 17.1mph/1000rpm in top gear.
Suspension and brakes: 11in-diameter drum brakes front and rear. 6.00–16-in tyres. Unladen weight 3330lb.
Performance: Not tested in this guise.
Price: £863 in 1945

Humber Super Snipe—produced 1945–48

Technical description: *The Autocar*, 3.8.45

Same chassis, suspension, and bodyshell as for 1945–48 Hawk, except for:
Engine: 6-cyl, 85 × 120mm, 4086cc, side valves, CR 6.3:1, Stromberg carb, 100bhp at 3400rpm.
Maximum torque 197lb ft at 1200rpm.
Transmission: Axle ratio 4.09:1. Overall ratios 4.09, 5.99, 10.14, 16.07, reverse 16.07:1. 19.7mph/1000rpm in top gear.
Suspension and brakes: 11in drum brakes at front and rear. 6.00–16in tyres. Unladen weight 3360lb.
Performance: (*The Autocar*, 13.12.46) Maximum speed 'over 75mph', 0–60mph 24.5sec. Typical fuel consumption 15–17mpg.
Price: £889 in 1945

Humber Super Snipe II—produced 1948–50

Technical description: *The Autocar*, 17.9.48

Same basic chassis, suspension, running gear and bodyshell as 1945–48 model, except for slightly lengthened wheelbase, wider tracks and body width, and restyled nose:
Transmission: Axle ratio 4.09:1. Overall ratios 4.09, 5.89, 9.59, 15.95, reverse 16.91:1. 20.25mph/1000rpm in top gear.

Suspension and brakes: 12in drum brakes at front and rear. 6.50–16in tyres. Unladen weight 3695lb.
Dimensions: Wheelbase 9ft 9.5in; front track 4ft 9.9in; rear track 5ft 1in. Length 15ft 7.5in; width 6ft 2.5in; height 5ft 5.7in.
Performance: (*The Autocar*, 23.5.49) Maximum speed 80mph. 0–60mph 22.7sec. Typical fuel consumption 14–18mpg.
Price: £1144 in 1948

Humber Super Snipe III—produced 1950–52

Technical description: *The Autocar*, 25.8.50

Same basic specification as for 1948–50 model except for:
Suspension and brakes: Rear suspension now has Panhard rod linkage. Overall length now quoted as 15ft 10.7in. Unladen weight 3745lb.
Price: £1144 in 1950
    £1240 in 1950 for 'Touring' limousine derivative

Replaced in October 1952 by new chassis/body design allied to 1948 variety of Humber Hawk.

Humber Pullman—produced 1945–48

Technical description: *The Autocar*, 3.8.45

Same basic chassis and mechanical layout as Hawk/Snipe/Super Snipe range, but with Thrupp & Maberly bodyshell, and following details:
Engine: As Super Snipe.
Transmission: As 1945–48 Super Snipe, except 20.2mph/1000rpm in top gear.
Suspension and brakes: 12in-diameter drum brakes front and rear. 6.50–16in tyres.
Dimensions: Wheelbase 10ft 7.5in; front track 4ft 7.8in; rear track 5ft 1in. Overall length 16ft 6in; width 6ft 1in; height 5ft 10in. Unladen weight 4005lb.
Performance: Not tested in this guise.
Price: £1598 in 1945

Humper Pullman II—produced 1948–53

Technical description: *The Autocar*, 28.5.48

Specification as for 1945–48 Pullman except for considerable styling changes and revised chassis as for Super Snipe II:
Suspension: 7.00–16in tyres.
Dimensions: Wheelbase 10ft 11in; front track 4ft 10in; rear track 5ft 2in. Overall length 17ft 6.5in; width 6ft 2.5in; height 5ft 9in. Unladen weight 4465lb.
Performance: (*The Autocar*, 4.7.52) Maximum speed 78mph. 0–60mph 26.2sec. Standing ¼-mile 23.2sec. Typical fuel consumption 14–17mpg.
Price: £2171 in 1948

Humber Pullman III—produced 1953 to 1954

Technical description: *The Autocar*, 8.5.53

Specification as for 1948–53 Pullman except for:
Engine: 6-cyl overhead-valve engine of 1952 Super Snipe (see below).
Suspension: 7.50–16in tyres.
Dimensions: Length now quoted as 17ft 7.9in.
Unladen weight 4870lb.
Performance: Never tested in this guise.
Price: £1977 in 1953

This model was dropped in 1954, and was never replaced.

Humber Imperial—produced 1949–53

Mechanically and visually this car was identical to the Pullman II of 1948–53, but fitted with a seven-seater arrangement without a limousine division.
Performance: (*The Autocar*, 21.10.49) Maximum speed 79mph. 0–60mph 26.5sec. Typical fuel consumption, about 13–15mpg.
Price: £2171 in 1949

Humber Imperial II—produced 1953–54

Mechanically and visually, this car was identical to the Pullman III of 1953–54, but fitted with a non-limousine variety of coachwork.
Unladen weight: 4845lb.
Performance: Not tested in this guise.
Price: £1977 in 1953

This model was dropped in 1954, and was never replaced.

Starting with the Humber Hawk announced in October 1948, Rootes ushered in a new range of Humbers. All 1948–57 Hawks, and all 1952–58 Super Snipes were based on the same basic chassis layout and pressed-body style, though there were significant differences in wheelbase, and in front and rear body sheet metal.

Humber Hawk III—produced 1948–50

Technical description: *The Autocar*, 15.10.48

Engine: 4-cyl, 75 × 110mm, 1944cc, side-valves, CR 6.4:1, Stromberg carb, 56bhp at 3800rpm. Maximum torque 97lb ft at 2000rpm.
Transmission: Axle ratio 4.55:1. Overall ratios 4.55, 6.78, 11.24, 16.14, reverse 21.62:1. 16.3mph/1000rpm in top gear.

MONTE CARLO RALLY

HUMBER

SUPER SNIPE

Drivers: M. Gatsonides & K. S. Barendregt

WINS

BARCLAY'S BANK CUP
FOR BEST PERFORMANCE
of any British Car

IRRESPECTIVE OF
PRICE OR HORSE-POWER

(Subject to official confirmation)

A PRODUCT OF THE ROOTES GROUP

At first glance the Humber won the rally? Advertizers' licence allows even more these days

---

Suspension and brakes: Ifs, coil springs, wishbones and lever-arm dampers; live rear axle, half-elliptic leaf springs, anti-roll bar, lever arm dampers. Worm and nut steering. 9in diameter drum brakes, front and rear. 5.50–15in tyres.
Dimensions: Wheelbase 8ft 9.5in; front track 4ft 8in; rear track 4ft 9in. Overall length 14ft 6in; width 5ft 10in; height 5ft 4in. Unladen weight 2750lb. Performance: (*The Autocar*, 15.7.49) Maximum speed 72mph. 0–60mph 34.4sec. Typical fuel consumption 24 to 27mpg.
Price: £799 in 1948.

Humber Hawk IV—produced 1950–52

Technical description: *The Autocar*, 25.8.50

Specification as for 1948–50 Hawk III except for:
Engine: 81 × 110mm, 2267cc, side-valves, CR 6.3:1,
58bhp at 3400rpm. Maximum torque 110lb ft at
1800rpm.
Transmission: 17.0mph/1000rpm in top gear.
Suspension and brakes: 6.40–15in tyres.
Performance: (*The Autocar*, 29.12.50) Maximum
speed 70mph. 0–60mph 30.4sec. Typical fuel
consumption 21–23mpg.

Humber Hawk V—produced 1952–54

Technical description: *The Autocar*, 26.9.52

Specification as for 1950–52 Hawk IV except for:
Transmission: Overall ratios 4.55, 6.78, 11.24, 14.50,
reverse 18.37:1.
Performance: Not tested in this guise.
Price: £1129 in 1952

Humber Hawk VI—produced 1954–57

Technical description: *The Autocar*, 11.6.54

Specification as for 1952–54 Hawk V except for:
Engine: Overhead valves, CR 7.0:1. 70bhp at
4000rpm. Maximum torque 119lb ft at 2200rpm.
Suspension and brakes: 4.5in wheel rims. Anti-roll bar
to front suspension. No anti-roll bar at rear. 10in
drum brakes all round.
Dimensions: Length now quoted as 15ft 1.5in
(without significant sheet metal changes). Unladen
weight 3110lb.
Options: (for export) 4.22:1 axle ratio. Overall ratios
4.22, 6.30, 10.43, 13.45, reverse 17.04:1.
Optional Laycock de Normanville overdrive with
4.55:1 axle ratio, giving overdrive top gear ratio of
3.54:1. 21.8mph/1000rpm in overdrive top gear.
Performance: (*The Autocar*, 13.8.54) Maximum speed
80mph in overdrive, 76mph in direct top gear.
0–60mph 23.8sec. Standing ¼-mile 22.5sec. Typical
fuel consumption about 22 to 31mpg.
Price: £986 in 1954

(Note: From September 1955, an estate car derivative
was made available. Specification was as for the saloon
except for:
Engine power now quoted as 75bhp at 4000rpm
(shared with saloon).
Tyres 6.00–15-in. Unladen weight 3360lb.
Price: £1255 in 1955)

Humber Super Snipe Mk IV—produced 1952–54

Technical description: *The Autocar*, 17.10.52

Engine: 6-cyl, 88.9 × 111.1mm, 4139cc, overhead
valves, CR 6.5:1, Stromberg carb, 113bhp at

3400rpm. Maximum torque 206lb ft at 1400rpm.
Transmission: Axle ratio 3.9:1. All-synchromesh
gearbox, overall ratios 3.9, 5.54, 8.16, 12.18, reverse
12.92:1. Alternative axle 3.7:1, overall ratios 3.7,
5.22, 7.74, 11.56, reverse 12.25:1. 21.3mph/1000rpm
in top gear or 22.5mph/1000rpm in top gear.
Suspension and brakes: Ifs, coil springs, wishbones,
anti-roll bar, telescopic dampers; live rear axle, half-
elliptic leaf springs, telescopic dampers. Worm and
nut steering. 11in-diameter drum brakes front and
rear. 7.00–15in tyres on 5.0in wheel rims.
Dimensions: Wheelbase 9ft 7.7-in; front track 4ft
10in; rear track 4ft 8.25in. Overall length 16ft 5in;
width 6ft 1.5in; height 5ft 6in. Unladen weight
4025lb.
Performance: (*The Autocar*, 29.5.53) Maximum speed
90mph. 0–60mph 16.0sec. Standing ¼-mile 20.5sec.
Typical fuel consumption 14 to 18mpg.
Price: £1627 in 1952

(Note: From autumn 1953, the engine was uprated,
with CR 7.1:1. 116bhp at 3500rpm. Maximum torque
211lb ft at 1400rpm.)

Humber Super Snipe Mk V—produced 1954–58

Technical description: *The Autocar*, 16.4.54

Specification as for uprated Super Snipe Mk IV
(1953–54 variety)
Performance: Never tested in this guise.
Price: £1397 in 1954

Note: From September 1955 the following engine
changes were introduced:
CR 7.4.1, 122bhp at 3600rpm.
Transmission: Axle ratio 4.1:1. Overall ratios 4.1,
5.82, 8.57, 12.8, reverse 13.57:1. Optional overdrive,
giving 3.2:1. 20.33mph/1000rpm in direct top gear,
26.0mph/1000rpm in overdrive top gear.
Performance: Not tested in this guise.
Price: £1552 in 1955

(Note: From April 1956, the car became available with
optional Borg Warner automatic transmission.
Price reductions also took place at this time:
£1426 (manual)
£1614 (automatic))

Starting with new Humber Hawk, announced in May
1957, and the new Super Snipe announced in October
1958, Rootes brought in a rationalized range of cars
all based on the same monocoque four-door bodyshell
which shared the same wheelbase, suspensions and
principal dimensions. Hawks had the old engine,
while Super Snipes and their derivatives had a
brand-new six-cylinder engine. These models carried
on until 1967, when both were phased out and not
replaced.

Humber Hawk—produced 1957–59

Technical description: *The Autocar*, 31.5.57

Engine: 4-cyl, 81 × 110mm, 2267cc, overhead valves, CR 7.5:1, Zenith carb, 73bhp (net) at 4400rpm. Maximum torque 120lb ft at 2300rpm.
Transmission: Manual, axle ratio 4.22:1, overall ratios 4.22, 6.30, 10.43, 13.46, reverse 17.04. Optional overdrive, axle ratio 4.56:1, overall ratios (3.54(, 4.56, 6.79, 11.26, 14.52, reverse 18.39. Optional automatic, axle ratio 4.22:1, overall ratios 4.22, 6.06, 9.79, reverse 8.48:1. 18.32mph/1000rpm in top gear (manual and automatic), 21.8mph/1000rpm in overdrive top gear.
Suspension: Ifs, coil springs, wishbones, anti-roll bar, telescopic dampers; live rear axle, half-elliptic leaf springs, telescopic dampers. Recirculating ball steering. 11in-diameter front drum brakes, 10in-diameter rear drum brakes. 6.00–15 or 6.40–15in tyres on 4.5in rims.
Dimensions: Wheelbase 9ft 2in; front track 4ft 8in; rear track 4ft 7.5in. Overall length 15ft 4.7in; width 5ft 9.5in; height 5ft 1in. Unladen weight 3080lb.
Performance: (*The Autocar*, 28.6.57) Maximum speed 83mph. 0–60mph 20.6sec. Standing ¼-mile 21.8sec. Typical fuel consumption about 25mpg.
Price: £1261 in 1957

(Note: An estate car derivative was introduced in October 1957, with only minor mechanical differences.)

Price: £1464 in 1957

Hawk Series 1A—produced 1959–60

Technical description: *The Autocar*, 16.10.59

Same basic mechanical specification except for:
Transmission: Overall ratios (manual) 4.22, 5.88, 9.04, 14.13, reverse 17.90. (Overdrive) (3.54), 4.55, 6.34, 9.75, 15.24, reverse 19.31:1.
Price: £1191 (saloon) in 1959
    £1411 (estate) in 1959

Hawk Series II—produced 1960–62

Technical description: *The Autocar*, 14.10.60

Same basic specification as Series 1A except for:
Transmission: Automatic transmission no longer available.
Suspension and brakes: 11.6in front disc brakes, 11in rear drums.
Price: £1241 (saloon) in 1960
    £1460 (estate) in 1960

Hawk Series III—produced 1962–64

Technical description: *The Autocar*, 14.9.62

Same basic specification as for Series II. Changes entirely cosmetic.
Price: £1204 (saloon) in 1962
    £1417 (estate) in 1962

Hawk Series IV—produced 1964–67

Technical description: *The Autocar*, 23.10.64

Same basic specification as for Series III, except for:
Suspension: Rear anti-roll bar, saloon version only.
Transmission: All-synchromesh gearbox, overall ratios 4.22, 5.88, 9.04, 14.16, reverse 15.07:1. Optional overdrive, ratio 3.28:1. 18.1mph/1000rpm in top gear, 23.3mph/1000rpm in overdrive top gear.
Performance: Not tested in this guise.
Price: £1095 (saloon) in 1964
    £1361 (estate) in 1964

Super Snipe—produced 1958–59

Technical description: *The Autocar*, 3.10.58

Same unit-construction four-door shell and suspensions as for Humber Hawk of 1957–67:
Engine: 6-cyl, 82.55 × 82.55mm, 2651cc, overhead valves, CR 7.5:1, Stromberg carb, 105bhp (net) at 5000rpm. Maximum torque 138lb ft at 2000rpm.
Transmission: Choice of manual, overdrive, or automatic transmission. Three-speed manual and automatic boxes. Axle ratio 4.55:1. Overall ratios (o/d top, if fitted, 3.54), 4.55, 7.34, 12.77, reverse 14.29:1. Automatic ratios 4.55, 6.5, 10.5, reverse 9.51:1. 17.4mph/1000rpm in top gear, 22.4mph/1000rpm in overdrive top gear.
Suspension: Ifs, coil springs, wishbones, anti-roll bar, telescopic dampers; live rear axles, half-elliptic leaf springs, telescopic dampers. Recirculating ball steering. 11in diameter front and rear drum brakes. 6.70–15in tyres.
Dimensions: Wheelbase 9ft 2in; front track 4ft 8.5in; rear track 4ft 7.5in. Overall length 15ft 4.75in; width 5ft 9.5in; height 5ft 1in. Unladen weight 3350lb.
Performance: (*The Autocar*, 31.10.58) Maximum speed 92mph (in overdrive), 87mph (direct top). 0–60mph 19.0sec. Standing ¼-mile 21.0sec. Typical fuel consumption 16 to 23mpg.
Price: £1494 (saloon) in 1958
    £1741 (estate) in 1958

Super Snipe Series II—produced 1959–60

Technical description: *The Autocar*, 16.10.59

Specification as for Super Snipe I except for:
Engine: 87.3 × 82.55mm, 2965cc, CR 8.0: 1, Zenith
carb. 121bhp (net) at 4800rpm. Maximum torque
162lb ft at 1800rpm.
Transmission: Automatic ratios 4.22, 6.03, 9.77,
reverse 8.82: 1. 18.5mph/1000rpm in top gear.
Brakes: 11in-diameter front discs, 11in-diameter rear
drums.
Performance: Not tested in this guise.
Price: £1453 (saloon) in 1959
　　　　£1701 (estate) in 1959

Super Snipe Series III—produced 1960–62

Technical description: *The Autocar*, 14.10.60

Specification as for Super Snipe II except for:
Overall length 15ft 8in.
Performance: (*The Autocar*, 16.6.61) Maximum speed
100mph (overdrive), 96mph (direct top). 0–60mph
14.3sec. Standing ¼-mile 19.5sec. Fuel consumption
between 15 and 26mph.
Price: £1489 (saloon) in 1960
　　　　£1737 (estate) in 1960

Super Snipe Series IV—produced 1962–64

Technical description: *The Autocar*, 14.9.62

Specification as for Super Snipe Series III except for:
Engine: 124bhp (net) at 5000rpm. Maximum torque
160lb ft at 2600rpm.
Transmission: Automatic ratios as before. Axle ratio
now 4.22: 1 on all derivatives. Manual ratios (3.28—
o/d), 4.22, 6.13, 11.83, reverse 13.25: 1. 18.6mph/
1000rpm in direct top gear and automatic, 23.9mph/
1000rpm in overdrive top gear.
Performance: Not tested in this guise.
Price: £1541 (saloon) in 1962
　　　　£1782 (estate) in 1962

Super Snipe Series V—produced 1964–67

Technical description: *The Autocar*, 23.10.64

Specification as for Super Snipe Series IV except for:
Engine: 2 Zenith-Stromberg carbs, 128.5bhp (net) at
5000rpm. Maximum torque 167lb ft at 2600rpm.
Power-assisted steering as standard. Rear anti-roll bar
for saloon cars.
Height 4ft 11.25in. Unladen weight 3415lb (saloon),
3495lb (estate).
Performance: Not tested in this guise—but see below.
Price: £1512 (saloon) in 1964
　　　　£1633 (estate) in 1964

Imperial—produced 1964–67

Technical description: *The Autocar*, 23.10.64

Mechanical specification in every way as for Super
Snipe Series V, except for standardization of
automatic transmission and Selectaride rear shock
absorbers. Manual or overdrive transmission not
available.
Estate car derivative not available.
Performance: (*The Autocar*, 11.6.65) Maximum speed
100mph. 0–60mph 16.2sec. Standing ¼-mile 20.7sec.
Typical fuel consumption 18mpg.
Price: £1796 (saloon in 1964)
　　　　£1917 (limousine) in 1964

(Note: 'Touring' limousine derivatives were also
available of all Hawks and Super Snipes in this series,
but they were mechanically identical.)

Appendix 4

Postwar Sunbeam Tiger prototypes

870: the initial version made from Series III Alpine; Warner T-10 gearbox,
3.07:1 rear axle ratio, rack-and-pinion steering, fabricated steering arms,
bulkhead/wheelarch panels, gearbox cover and experimental radiator.

AF1: (designation stands for 'Alpine-Ford'). Alpine Series IV body, Le Mans
racing car. Later AFs used Alpine Series IV bodies entirely.

AF2: rough road (MIRA) test vehicle.

AF3: shipped to Shelby, Venice, for US racing preparation.

AF4: durability test car, Rootes-Coventry.

AF5: durability test car, Rootes-Coventry.

AF6: test car for Jensen Motors, West Bromwich.

AF7: test car for Humber: brake development. Rear axle ratio here changed to
2.88:1; handbrake was deemed adequate.

AF8: first show model, New York Automobile Show.

AF9: first pre-production prototype with all modifications intact, left-hand
drive.

AF10: second pre-production prototype, left-hand drive.

AF11: third pre-production prototype, right-hand drive, later tested with 289
engine, later used for disc brake testing.

AF12: fourth pre-production prototype, right-hand drive.

AF1 : not assigned.

AF14: test vehicle for automatic transmission.

AF15: test vehicle for brake servo.

AF201: first prototype Tiger II, with 260 engine.

AF202: second prototype Tiger II, with automatic transmission.

AF203: third prototype Tiger II, with 289 engine; for silencer testing.

AF204: fourth prototype Tiger II, 289 engine; alternator testing.

AF205: fifth prototype Tiger II, tyre testing.

AF206: sixth prototype Tiger II, test car, Rootes-Coventry.

AF207: seventh prototype Tiger II, Technical Department, Coventry.

Ten	1945–48	4719	'New' Super Snipe	1959		n.a.
2-litre	1945–58	1124	Super Snipe II	1960		n.a.
80	1949–50	3500	Super Snipe III	1961–62		7257
90 Mark I	1949–50	4000	Pullman II	1949		1083
90 Mark II	1951	5493	Pullman II	1950		833
90 Mark IIa	1952	4312	Pullman II	1951		907
	1953	n.a.	Pullman II	1952–53		620
	1954	n.a.	Super Snipe IV	1963–64		6495
Series III	1955–57	n.a.	Super Snipe V	1965		n.a.
Alpine Mark I	1953–54	n.a.	Super Snipe Va	1965–67		1731
Alpine Mark II	1955	n.a.	Imperial V	1965–67	est.	1200
			Imperial Va	1965–67		1125

Rapier

Mark I	1956	3375
Mark I R67	1957	3526
Mark II	1958	n.a.
Mark III	1959	n.a.
Mark III	1960	11,643
	1961	3850
	1962–63	17,534

(Note: Some Series V Imperials were registered as late as 1967; this may also have occurred on Series V Super Snipes. The Series Va was instituted only when Rootes changed its serialization sequences.)

* Sunbeam Tiger production figures are subject to date. The stop and start of production of each series was as follows:

Model	Start	Stop
Mk I	27 Jun 64— B9470001	6 Aug 65— B9473756
Mk Ia	7 Aug 65— B382000001	9 Dec 66— B382002694
Mk II	10 Dec 66— B382100001	30 Jun 67— B382100633

Alpine

Series I	1960	11,904
Series II	1961–63	19,956
Series III	1963–64	5863
Series IV	1964–66	12,406
Series V	1966–68	19,122

Tiger*

Mark I	1964–65	4669
Mark Ia	1966	1826
Mark II	1967–68	571

Our Mark I start date is based on Gregory Wells's research in *Special-Interest Autos*; other sources state as early as 19 March. The final Mark I figure is Mike Taylor's; another source has it as B9473762. Taylor also lists the first Mark II as B382100100, but B382100001 has been found in North Carolina! (And if Taylor's start figure is accepted, more Tigers were sold than built.) Taylor's stop date for the Mark II is 27 June, but other sources all say 30 June. Correctly, our table is a shipping total, 7067 units. The above stop-start dates total 7083 units, the 16-car difference believed to be factory sales or executive cars. It is possible, too, that some of these 16 were competition Tigers.

Humber**

Hawk IV	1951	8866
Hawk VI	1956	6061
'New' Hawk	1957	1501
Hawk II	1961–62	6974
Super Snipe III	1951	4397
Super Snipe IV	1953–54	4200
Super Snipe V	1955–56	1268

Appendix 6
Bibliography

Books:
Titles consulted for research purposes for this book. All must be considered as further reading on the cars of the Rootes Group.

Carroll: *Tiger, An Exceptional Motorcar*, Sports Car Press.

Culshaw/Horrobin: *Complete Catalogue of British Cars*, Morrow 1974.

Dalton: *Those Elegant Rolls-Royce*, Dalton-Watson 1967 and subseq.

Frostick: *Works Team*, Cassell 1964.

Georgano: *The Complete Encyclopedia of Motorcars*, Dutton 1968 and subseq.; *Encyclopedia of Motor Sport*, Viking 1971.

Langworth: *Studebaker, The Postwar Years*, Motorbooks International 1979.

Langworth/Robson: *Triumph Cars*, Motor Racing Publications 1979.

McGovern: *Alpine, The Classic Sunbeam*, Gentry Books 1980.

Olyslager: *British Cars of the Early Thirties/Late Thirties/Early Forties/Late Forties/Early Fifties/Late Fifties*, Warne 1973 and subseq.

Taylor: *Tiger, The Making of a Sports Car*, Gentry Books 1980.

Periodicals:
Numerous editions of the following periodicals were also consulted.
Autocar, Car and Driver, Car Classics, Motor, Motor Sport, Road & Track, Sports Car Graphic, Sports Cars Illustrated, Thoroughbred & Classic Cars, Today's Motor Sports, The Milestone Car.

Index